Holiday Quilts

Barbara Campbell and Yolanda Fundora

©2007 Barbara Campbell and Yolanda Fundora
Published by

kp **krause publications**
An Imprint of F+W Publications

700 East State Street • Iola, WI 54990-0001
715-445-2214 • 888-457-2873
www.krausebooks.com

Our toll-free number to place an order or obtain
a free catalog is (800) 258-0929.

The following registered trademark terms and companies appear in this publication: Mountain Mist®, Stitch Witchery®, Teflon™, The Bottom Line™, The MasterPiece™, Timtex™, iPod

Library of Congress Catalog Number: 2006935442

ISBN 978-0-89689-482-2

Designed by Heidi Bittner-Zastrow
Edited by Tracy L. Conradt

Acknowledgments

❄ From the Quilter's Point of View

Since this has been a collaborative effort, we felt it was appropriate to give you our thoughts and acknowledgments from two separate points of view. There are so many people to thank on my journey to this book. First, and foremost, my gratitude goes to my husband (and best friend), Gary, for his support that allowed me to follow my dream. Then there are my sons, Gary Scott and Brian and their wives, Chris and Diane, who have become two of my best friends, for believing in and encouraging me. My grandkids lift me up with their love and admiration. I am now teaching three of them the basics of sewing, including my 10-year-old grandson, Scott. Caitlyn, who is 8, has just finished making her first charm square quilt after hand sewing a "sleepover pillow." Juliet, at 6, helped me paint some special fabric and sew it into a small doll's quilt. Sarah is just 3, but showing a lot of interest in the fabrics and pins already. Here's to the next generation of quilters!

I have met so many inspirational quilters along the way that it's hard to single anyone out for recognition. The first one that comes to mind is one of my best friends, Shirley Giampoala, who convinced me to try cutting up fabric into tiny little pieces and sewing them back together, something I resisted for a long time. The credit for influencing me to purchase my first Bernina goes to my cousin-in-law and good friend, Jan Wargo. Once I made the purchase I felt the need to justify it, so I bought some fabric, attended my first quilting class with Shirley (a stack-n-whack) and made my husband a lap quilt. The rest, as they say, is history.

Attending quilt shows became a passion and I met and became friends with Elle Colquitt Speer (formerly of The Picket Fence Quilt Design pattern company). Volunteering to help make some of her booth samples led to her recommendation for me to make a Quilt Market sample for one of the fabric companies. Nancy Alemdar gave me the opportunity to design something using the fabrics she designed for Balson-Erlanger. That quilt attracted the attention of Candy Wiza (former editor of Better Homes and Gardens Quilt Catalog and current Acquisitions Editor for Krause Publications). Candy purchased several of my patterns for sale in that catalog and officially started my pattern design business. That relationship led me here — to my first quilt book.

Along the way, I picked up not only quilting techniques and skills from some very accomplished quilters, but also technical reading, pattern writing and editing skills from Laurette Koserowski, Editorial Director for the quilting publications of All American Crafts. She has been publishing my quilt designs for several years and has always been very generous in sharing her expertise. My friendship with Jacqui Clarkson, an accomplished needle artist, opened the door for appreciating handwork. We partnered on many published projects with coordinating hand and machine work, including a book for Jeanette Crews titled "Denim Divas." There are many other quilters who have shared, supported and encouraged me along the way, including my local friends who stepped in to help get this book to press on time — Karen Anderson, Sue Mangina, Jennifer Roth, Carol Singer and Patti Welch.

The timely delivery of this book and these projects could not have been accomplished without the support of my favorite dealer, Pocono Sew & Vac, in Stroudsburg, Pa. As part of their continuing outstanding customer service, they have come to the rescue and serviced my ailing machine in record time. Broken needles jammed in the hook system were no challenge for their crackerjack technician. Thanks guys!

A great big thanks and appreciation go to my creative business partner, Yolanda Fundora. She adds the artistic and product developmental skills to my sewing and quilting background to create an unbelievable collaboration. Together we have found the perfect complement to achieve what we have both been dreaming and searching for.

Thanks to all my friends and mentors in the quilting industry for helping to guide me along the way. It has been a magnificent journey and I look forward to continuing to grow and learn with all of you.

Finally, we both want to show our appreciation to all the people at Windham Fabrics for believing in this project enough to print a special line of holiday fabrics for it and to the folks at Krause for the opportunity to put together this book.

— Barbara

❄ From the Textile Designer's Point of View

All artists in all media create to share what they see and feel with others. In my life, my fine art work is inextricably intertwined with my design work, so there are many people to thank in both the fine art and commercial worlds. I have been fortunate to encounter many people in my life that have been instrumental in setting me along the path I walk so happily now.

My deepest thanks goes to my parents, Mario and Yolanda Fundora. They not only sacrificed financially to make sure I got all the art training I needed very early in life, but also showed through example how much happiness creativity and artistic expression can bring to your life.

Cheryl Johnson, Scott McIntire, Peggy Karr, and Cynthia Hart are people who, throughout my design career, have worked closely with me and have been instrumental in fine-tuning my personal design aesthetic. In the fine art world, much appreciation goes to Dr. María Emilia Somoza, director of the Museum of Contemporary Art of Puerto Rico, for offering me her support throughout the years in the form of solo and group exhibitions at the museum.

Barbara and I were happy to enjoy the generous and visionary support of Mickey Krueger of Windham Fabrics, whose collaboration in printing our holiday fabrics way ahead of schedule has allowed us to write an even better book.

Above all I have to thank my life partner, Pamela Zave, research scientist and art quilter, for her belief in my talent and her total commitment and support every day and every step of the way. When I sit down to design a line of fabric, seeing Pamela intent on making whatever quilt she is working on the very best she has ever done, I cannot help but to try to do the same.

— Yolanda

Table of Contents

OUR UNPLANNED JOURNEY
by Barbara Campbell & Yolanda Fundora

Yolanda's Story

A passion for art manifested itself very early in my life. My mother tells me of my four-year-old's refusal to move from the window of an art supply store in Old Havana until the rainbow box of Prismacolor pencils in the window was procured. I also have a vivid recollection of being chastised for removing everything from my kindergarten satchel except blank pieces of paper, a series of carrot drawings, and my Prismacolor box. I needed to see some vague "someone" to show them my "portfolio." How this idea of the workings of the art world had come to a four-year-old is unfathomable now, but somehow my imagination had converted my kindergarten teacher into an important art dealer.

In 1961, a few years after the Prismacolor episode, my parents and I emigrated to New York City, where family awaited us. In New York my art education began in earnest. In fourth grade a retiring art teacher, perhaps recognizing a kindred spirit, decided to take me under her wing. She determinedly prepared me for entering every single contest available to my age group that year. Wanting to make her last year as an art teacher one for both of us to remember, she got special permission from the school and spent an entire day with me sitting on the Great Lawn in Central Park. She parked me with all her personal art supplies and made me draw the same scene (the twin towers of a building on 75th and Central Park West—an orienting beacon for West Siders walking in the park) over and over in all the media I could handle at the time: charcoal, oil pastel, my beloved Prismacolors, and chalk pastel. We won seven gold medals and one silver that year in Manhattan and New York City All-Borough art contests, one in every category we entered.

My parents could no longer doubt that art would play an important role in my life, and made sure I got all the technical art education possible from then on. I had private after-school lessons and frequent trips to the Metropolitan Museum of Art and Museum of Modern Art.

Fabric design and quilting found me much later in my artistic career. I moved to Puerto Rico in 1981 both to regain my Hispanic cultural heritage and to pursue my fine art. While there my work caught the eye of recruiters for a design studio to be dually-based in New York City and San Juan. I moved back to New York in 1991 and entered a new phase of my career, licensing designs for both three-dimensional and surface-design products.

I learned to design for textiles through having to adapt some of my illustrations for use on home-décor fabrics. I discovered that I deeply enjoyed this area of commercial design. A long and rewarding period of both licensed and freelance work with some of the major textile companies followed, VIP/Cranston, Concord Windham, and Free Spirit among them.

In the last few years, my intense love of fabric design has led me more and more to seek and enjoy the company of quilters. Through my membership in the Garden State Quilters, I was very fortunate to meet Barbara Campbell, whose quilting design and publishing expertise has been a welcome complement to my fabric design and illustration skills. Currently Barbara and I work together designing fabrics and quilts. We combine our broad-based experience to bring fabric lines to market that quilters can enjoy and use successfully to create their own works of art.

Barbara's Story

Little did I know when a dear friend convinced me to try my hand at quilting several years ago that I would find myself immersed in a new career. I have always sewn, starting in grade school and continuing into adulthood, making clothing, baby and home décor items. My interests have spanned most all the handcrafts, usually making items to embellish my home.

I have enjoyed meeting and taking classes with some very special teachers in the quilt world. Traveling to many quilt shows has given me the opportunity to make friends with quilters, shop owners, vendors and designers. I have been very lucky in the direction my life has taken, and met so many wonderful people in this industry.

Given the opportunity to work as a Technical Reader for *The Quilter Magazine*, a whole new world opened for me. Thanks to the friendship and guidance I have found there, I was ready for the challenges presented by the opportunity to edit two new quilting magazines.

Editing *Quilts & Coordinates* married my love of quilting with my interest in home decorating.

Fabric Trends magazine gave me an opportunity to work with the newest fabrics introduced to quilters. I was privileged to work with many established as well as up-and-coming designers in putting together several wonderful issues.

As change seems to be the constant in my life, I am once again happily designing and sewing quilts. I enjoy working with the fabric manufacturers in designing contemporary quilts, using their latest fabrics. I have also been fortunate in having many of my designs published in magazines and catalogs, and my teaching and pattern business has begun. All this has led me to working with my good friend and business partner, Yolanda Fundora, and designing the projects for this book and collaborating on new fabric designs. Getting to know each other through our local quilt guild, Garden State Quilters in Chatham, New Jersey, we feel very lucky to have found the opportunity to work together and look forward to sharing many creative years. ☺

Conclusion

We can't wait to see how this new path evolves for us and hope that you will enjoy making the projects we have put together for this holiday/everyday book as much as we have enjoyed creating them. Our goal was to create patterns that could easily be used to coordinate many of the rooms in your home. Hopefully by showing the same projects done in both holiday and everyday fabrics, you will be inspired to use different colorways with the same basic patterns to create totally different looks for year-round use. Have fun with the dimensional pieces and make lots of Jumping Jacks for all your little friends. The kids we showed them to were all fascinated. ☺

Basic Quilting Lessons

There are many different ways of approaching the cutting, piecing, appliqué and quilting techniques today. Below are directions and suggestions that we find helpful in creating our projects quickly and easily. We suggest that beginners consider taking introductory lessons at their local quilt shops for more detailed instructions.

Equipment

It is important to have the best equipment you can afford and to keep it in good operating condition.

Sewing Machine

Your sewing machine should be cleaned and oiled regularly for the best results. Become familiar with its features and operations. A yearly professional service is recommended as part of the regular maintenance of your machine. If you have questions about its operation that cannot be answered in your operator's manual, your local dealer can be a great resource. The most important piece of advice for you to be aware of is not to sew over pins in your work. This practice can result in personal injury or damage to your sewing machine.

Keep your sewing machine covered when not in use. Change needles frequently as it is important to use a sharp needle when piecing and quilting.

If there is a walking foot available for your sewing machine, it can be a valuable tool when sewing long strips or quilting in the ditch to help feed the layers evenly. You should explore other specialty feet which can make your work easier. Check with your sewing machine dealer to see what feet they recommend for specific tasks. An accurate ¼" foot can be invaluable in piecing.

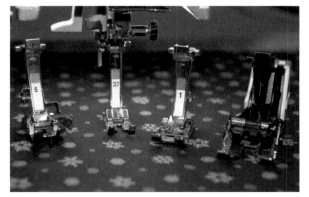

Having specialty feet on hand for your sewing machine can make piecing and quilting easier.

Rotary Cutters

Most quilters are familiar with rotary cutting techniques and tools. There are many on the market today to choose from, including some that are designed with ergonomics in mind. Your local quilt shop can help you determine which type of cutter would work best for you.

It is very important to use a sharp blade for accuracy when cutting fabric. There are tools available to sharpen and extend the life of your rotary blade, but you should always keep extra replacement blades on hand. The blades can become nicked or dull and need to be replaced. Follow manufacturer's instructions to dismantel and replace the blade with care.

Always cover the blade when not in use, even if you are putting your rotary cutter down for "just a minute." Accidents can happen much too easily with these razor sharp tools.

Rulers and Templates

There are many choices on the market today for rulers to help in rotary cutting your quilt pieces. We suggest purchasing rulers with clear markings that are easy to see when lining up with your fabric. Also helpful is the non-skid backing that is imprinted into the back of some brands. In lieu of that, you can find small sandpaper or vinyl peel-and-stick "dots" that can adhere to the backside of the rulers. This helps to keep your ruler in place as you rotary cut the fabric. In addition, there is a vinyl sheet that can be cut to the correct size for your various rulers. It uses static to cling to the back of the rulers to create the non-skid surface.

Acrylic templates can also be treated with these products to help keep them secure when cutting.

We have found template plastic to be invaluable in making pattern pieces, especially if they will be used over again.

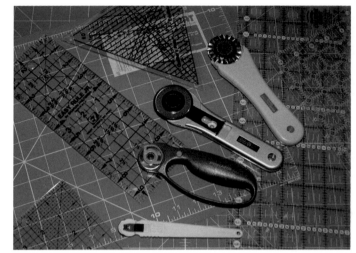

There are many brands and sizes to choose from in cutting mats, rotary cutters, rulers and templates.

Fold the fabric along the length twice, making sure it is straight, and trim one edge to square it up. Determine the width of strips to cut, and use the appropriate size ruler to cut them.

Use a permanent marker to trace over your pattern shape and cut the template with scissors, if curved, or with a rotary cutter if it has straight edges. Always mark your template with the project name and piece number for future reference. If making templates for appliqué, include the seam allowance if using a hand appliqué method. If you intend to use a fusible method for machine appliqué, do not include the seam allowance.

Cutting Mats

Today there are also many types of cutting mats you can use. Most important to consider are a smooth cutting surface and accurate measurements. We suggest having one large mat (24" x 36") for doing most of your strip cutting. It is also helpful to have a smaller mat to take to class and to use when you need to turn fabric to trim additional edges. By turning the mat instead of disturbing the cut fabric, you will increase the accuracy of your pattern pieces.

Fabric

Most quilting projects suggest using good quality 100-percent cotton fabrics. Fabrics should be pre-washed if you suspect that the colors may run. You can test a small piece by submerging in hot water to see if the colors are permanent. Many people like to pre-wash and press all their fabrics before beginning any project. We have taken into consideration that fabrics may shrink and have allowed extra fabric in our materials lists to account for that.

In order to cut accurate strips, fold the fabric lengthwise in half and press. Fold again, matching up the edges. Trim the raw edge to square up the length of fabric and begin cutting the correct size strips with your rotary cutter and ruler. It is important to cut your pieces on the straight of grain as much as possible. The exception is when cutting bias strips for binding or piecing curves. Then you would want to cut the fabric on a 45-degree angle, which allows a little stretch to accommodate curves.

Thread

Depending on the type of project you are working on, there are many different types and weights of thread available. We prefer using a 50-weight bobbin thread in the bobbin whenever possible, including our new favorite — pre-wound bobbins. We try to match the color closely with the fabric. If you use heavier threads, you might have to adjust your upper tension and use a 90/14 or 100/16 topstitch or metallic needle, which have larger eyes and do not tend to shred thicker threads. Experiment with your sewing machine and different types of thread to determine your preferences. We have used cotton, polyester, rayon and blends in these projects. You can achieve some wonderful decorative results with the variegated and metallic threads which are readily available. Have fun trying different types for different looks.

Be careful, thread addiction can be as contagious as fabric addiction.

Sewing

We offer tips and tricks for readers who are familiar with their machines. It is very important to get to know the features of your sewing machine. Read your manual and practice to achieve accurate sewing techniques.

Piecing

Unless otherwise noted, use a ¼" seam allowance throughout. Sew all pieces with right sides together and raw edges even, using coordinating thread. Refer to individual project instructions for detailed sewing techniques where applicable.

The most important part of the sewing process in quilting is accuracy. Most patterns, unless otherwise noted, use a ¼" seam allowance. It is important to check to make sure your seam allowance is accurate. Cut two pieces of fabric to measure 1¾" x 6". Sew them together along the 6" side. Press the seam allowance to one side and measure the finished piece. It should measure 3" x 6". If your piece is larger or smaller, adjust your stitching to achieve the correct measurement. It might be helpful to mark the correct placement of your fabric on the bed of your machine, or make an indication on the presser foot so you can be consistent in your ¼" seam allowance.

The next thing to consider is pressing your seam allowances. It is customary to press toward the darker fabric. When joining pieced units together, it is helpful to have the joining seams pressed in opposing directions so that they "nest" together. This will assure that your seams and points will come together accurately. We also suggest pressing the final seams open when many seamed edges come together in a block.

Chain piecing is a valuable time saver. Whenever possible, stitch like units for your project at the same time, using a scrap of fabric to start and stop your chain. Using a needle down position, if possible, start sewing with your fabric scrap, followed by the first unit. Stop at the edge of that unit, but do not raise the needle. Raise the presser foot slightly and insert the next unit, leaving a small space in between the first and second units. Lower the presser foot and continue sewing. Repeat until you have all the like units stitched in a chain. Remove from the machine and clip the connecting threads. Press the seams and continue this process until all individual units are pieced. This same process can be used to join the units and assemble the blocks for your project.

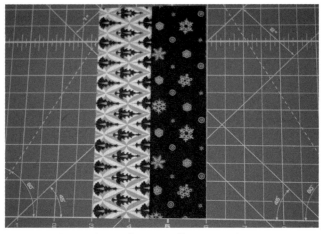

Accuracy in sewing ¼" seam allowances is important in quilting projects.

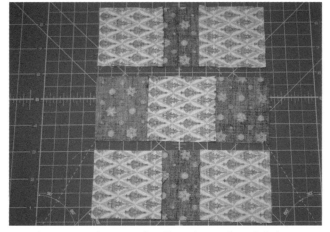

Pressing seams in opposite directions when joining units encourages all the individual pieces to line up.

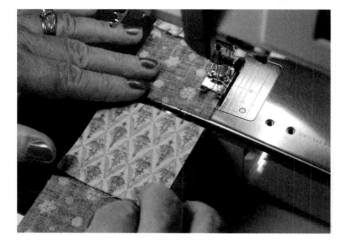

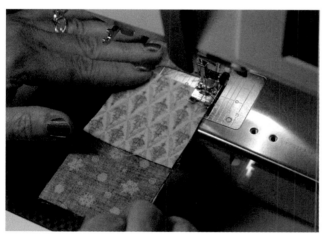

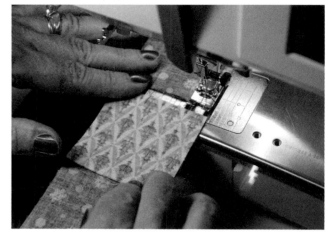

Chain piecing can save a lot of time by sewing units together in assembly line fashion.

Appliqué

The appliqué projects in this book have all been done with a fusible, machine appliqué process. There are many books available on hand appliqué for those who do not wish to use fusibles or a sewing machine to appliqué their designs. When preparing pattern pieces for hand appliqué, it is important to include a seam allowance. When using a fusible web to apply your pattern piece, the seam allowance is eliminated. It is also important to reverse your pattern pieces when using fusible web, as the web is fused to the wrong side of the fabric.

When using fusible web for machine appliqué trace the patterns on the paper side and in reverse if they are not symmetrical. Loosely cut the shape out, leaving at least ¼" around the drawn edges.

Follow the manufacturer's instructions for applying the web to the wrong side of the fabric. Cut each pattern piece on the drawn lines and remove the backing paper. Position the piece on your project and press in place, following temperature and time suggestions by the manufacturer.

We strongly suggest using a Teflon or silicon pressing sheet when working with fusible products. It will protect both your iron and your ironing surface. There are many brands and sizes available.

You can stitch just inside the appliqué shape using free motion for raw-edge appliqué. With this technique, you can try using coordinating threads or invisible thread, depending on the look that appeals to you. Another option is to satin stitch with a coordinating thread around all outside edges for a more pristine look. To achieve a primitive look, use a buttonhole stitch or zigzag and a contrasting thread.

Finishing Your Quilt

For adding borders, layering your quilt, binding and adding your identifying label, once again you can choose from several different methods. What we have suggested below is for readers who intend to machine quilt their projects. Once again, if you decide to hand quilt, there are many books available on that topic.

Borders

Once your quilt top is assembled, measure through the center in both horizontal and vertical directions. Use these measurements to calculate the length of borders to cut. Since fabric stretches, there is a possibility that all edges will not measure exactly the same as what the pattern suggests. Find the center of your quilt top on all edges and mark. Also, mark the center of your border strips. Pin the centers and the corners. Finally, pin from the center to the outside, easing the border to fit. Sew in place, with the fullness (if any) on the underside, so that your feed dogs will help to ease the fit.

Layering & Quilting

In most quilting books, magazines and patterns the dreaded words "quilt as desired" are all the instructions provide. In this book, we have tried to offer suggestions about what and how to quilt each piece. We are also assuming that readers will be quilting on their home machines. If you decide to quilt on a long-arm system, follow the manufacturer's instructions for loading your project on the quilt frame.

Make sure the batting and backing fabric are at least 2" - 3" larger all around than your quilt top. If piecing the backing, we suggest pressing the seam open to reduce the bulk in that area. If using a domestic machine to quilt, start in the center and quilt toward the outer edges. Once the quilting is complete, remove any remaining pins and basting

If Teflon or silicon sheets are not available in your area, you can substitute parchment paper to protect your iron and ironing surface.

thread and trim the excess batting and backing to square it up.

Pin or Thread Basting

Lay the backing fabric wrong side up on a flat surface. Tape in place, if possible. We often use a ceramic tile floor, as it allows us to line up with the tiles so that everything is straight and accurate. Place the batting on top of the backing, smoothing in place. Finally, center the quilt top, smooth in place and use small safety pins to pin the quilt every 3" - 4", according to the manufacturer's suggestions for the particular batting you are using. If you decide to thread baste, use a long running stitch in rows about 3" - 4" apart in both horizontal and vertical directions.

Adhesive Spray Basting

Lay the backing fabric wrong side up on a flat surface. Tape in place, if possible. Again, a tile floor is useful in aligning everything. Place the batting on top of the backing, smoothing in place. Lift the batting and roll back half way. Spray the backing fabric and begin to roll the batting back in place, smoothing as you go. Repeat for the other half. Finally, center the quilt top, smooth in place and repeat the process, rolling back the quilt top half way and spraying the batting surface.

Alternative Pillowcase Method of Layering

For those who wish to finish their projects without applying a binding, you can layer the batting, backing with right side up and the quilt top, wrong side up. In this case, the batting and backing will be cut the same size as the finished quilt top. Stitch all edges ¼" from the outside of the quilt top, leaving an opening to turn. Trim the batting and backing even with the quilt top. Turn to the right side and stitch the edge closed. Quilt the top in the ditch around the blocks to stabilize and then use a decorative quilting design where desired. This method is also referred to as "birthing."

Another suggestion is to layer the batting and quilt top, right side up, baste and do the detailed quilting as desired. Then layer the backing and quilt top right sides together and stitch around the edges, leaving the opening to turn. Turn to the right side and stitch the edge closed. Quilt the top in the ditch around blocks and in borders to secure.

Binding

In most cases, we suggest cutting your binding at 2". This seems to be the preferred width by most quilt judges at today's quilt shows. They feel that the binding is more likely to be filled when cut at this size. There are two methods we have used for binding the finished projects. In both cases the corners are mitered, which will be described below.

Prepare your binding strips by cutting enough 2" by width of fabrics to join together to cover the outside circumference of your quilt, plus at least 6". For a 60"-square quilt, that would mean four times 60", equaling 240" plus 6", divided by 40" (usable width of most fabrics), which gives you exactly six strips to cut.

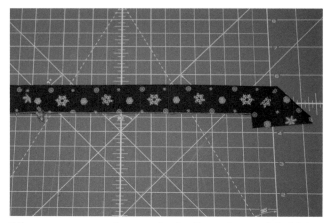

There are many other methods of starting and finishing the binding on quilts.

Piece the strips together by joining them right sides together with the edges at right angles and sewing a ∠5-degree angle across them. Trim seam allowance and press open.

Continue piecing strips until you have enough to go around your entire quilt, with a few inches to spare. Fold the binding strip in half lengthwise and press. Fold the corner of one end at a 45-degree angle and press. Trim points where the strips join and excess at the end of the strip where folded down.

The first method is fairly traditional. Place the binding strip, raw edges together, on top of the right side of the quilt: the folded edge will face the inside of the quilt. Using a ¼" seam allowance, begin sewing the binding strip in the middle of one side of the quilt, leaving a few inches of binding unsewn. Continue sewing around all the edges, mitering the corners until you come within a few inches of where you started (see mitering instructions). When you reach your starting point, trim the long end of the remaining binding strip on a 45-degree angle to a few inches so it will tuck into the folded starting end of the binding.

Carefully pin the two ends in place, and continue stitching until all the binding is secure. Turn

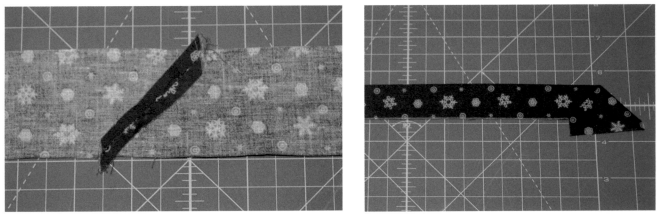

Seaming on a 45-degree angle makes the joints of the binding less obvious.

the quilt over to the wrong side, fold the binding over to the back and hand stitch to the back of the quilt.

The second method involves machine sewing both the front and back of the binding. Begin by sewing the binding to the back of the quilt with the same technique described above for the front. You will again miter the corners and finish the ends the same way. Turn the folded binding edge to the front of the quilt and use a zigzag or decorative stitch to sew it down, just covering the previous stitching line. This adds an additional decorative element to the finished project.

Mitering Corners

Pin the binding in place and stitch to ¼" from the edge of the side. It is helpful to place a pin at the intersection where you intend to stop stitching. Backstitch to secure.

Most of the mitered corners you will work with are 90-degree angles at the four corners of the quilt. Mitering can be done, however, on any angle whether concave or convex.

Lift the presser foot and fold the binding strip away from you, lining it up with the next edge to sew.

Fold the binding strip down over itself, creating a mitered corner and pin in place. Start sewing from the beginning of the corner.

Fold over to the other side of the quilt, pin in place and hand or machine stitch, being careful to create a miter in each of the corners on this side, as well.

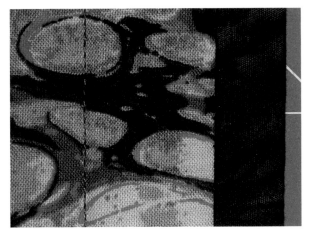

Though it is more time consuming, hand stitching the folded binding to the back of the quilt is still the favored method by most quilters.

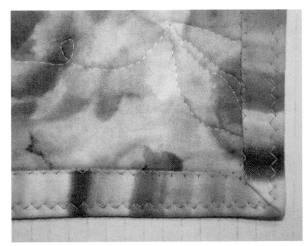

This method not only secures the binding edge, but also provides another decorative element to your quilted piece.

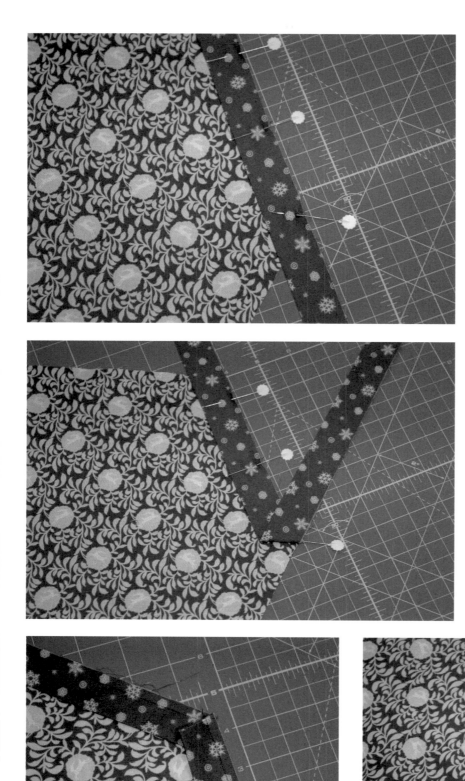

Careful pinning and sewing are important in this method.

Hanging sleeves are usually required whenever a quilt is entered into a show. They are also handy when displaying quilts in your home, making it easy to slip a dowel or rod into and avoiding damage to the quilt backing.

Hanging Sleeve

If you plan to hang your quilt on a wall or enter it into a quilt show, a hanging sleeve is required. Measure the width of your quilt and cut your sleeve 9" by that measurement. You may have to piece the sleeve for a larger quilt. Turn in the short ends ¼" and press. Turn in another ¼" and press again. Stitch to secure. If you are using the first traditional method for binding your quilt, line up the sleeve on the top of the quilt before you sew on the binding. Pin in place and stitch it along with the binding. If you are using the second method of machine stitching both sides, apply the binding first and then position the sleeve as shown alone and pin in place. Stitch in the ditch from the front side, using invisible thread in the top and bobbin. Once the top edge is sewn, no matter which method you are using, hand stitch the bottom of the sleeve in place.

Several different types of labels are pictured here to give you some ideas about how to create one for your masterpieces.

Label

It is very important to label your finished quilt, whether you are planning to give it as a gift or keep it for yourself. Future generations of quilters and historians will be pleased to have the information about who made the quilt, when and where it was made, if there was a special reason or celebration for its creation and whatever other history you can include. You can use a permanent fabric marker on a plain, light-colored fabric to write your information. Another option is to use a word processing or layout software to create a more sophisticated label and print it directly on fabric. You can also purchase label making software to create some fancier labels. Use some of your leftover fabric from the quilt to sew a small border on the label. So make your label, hand stitch to the back and display your finished works of art with pride.

The Family Room

Imagine celebrating your holiday in a coordinated room setting.
The projects provided here will help pull your decorations together for a designer look.
Make a tree skirt or table topper that coordinates with your lap quilt. Use the same pattern for the mantel
cover to create a window valance. Small pieces of leftover fabric can be used for the dimensional accessories.
You can create a year-round custom look by choosing everyday fabrics to complement your décor.

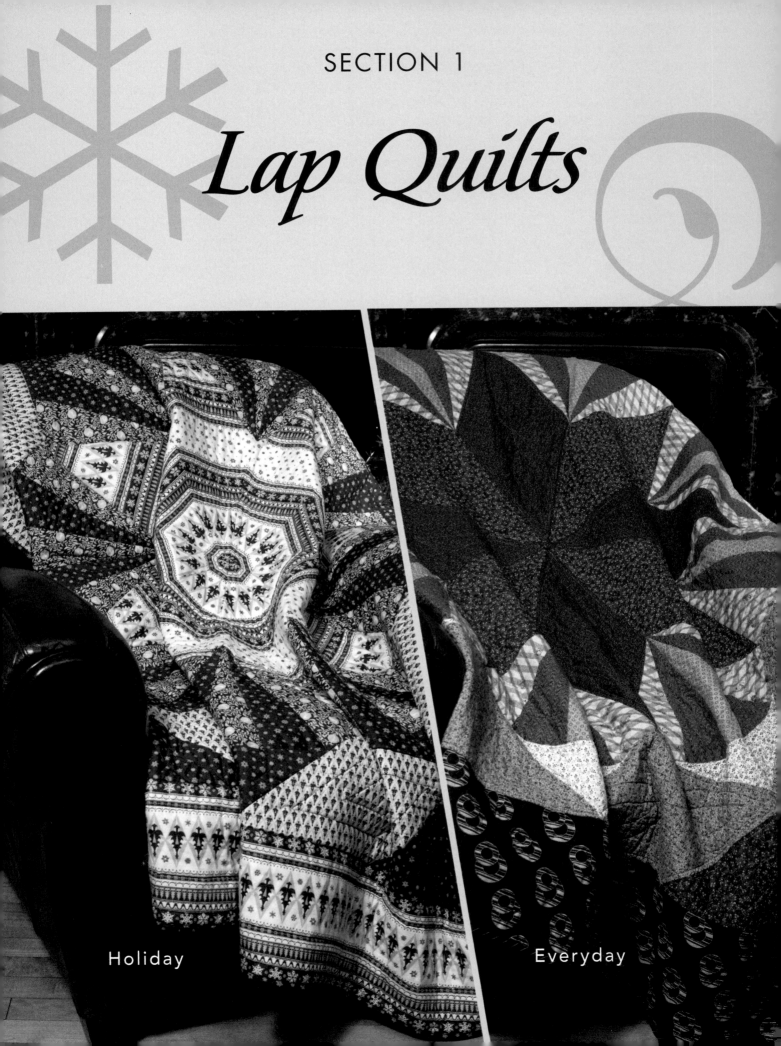

Lap Quilts

Holiday

Everyday

You can create a lap quilt with a snowflake effect by using a festive border print and combining some of the fan blades with the background fabric. Use inset techniques to sew the fan blocks to the background diamonds. Careful marking and pinning make the process simple with these large pieces. The snowflake design is suggested by using the same background fabric as some of the fan blades. By changing the placement of the colors on the fan blades and using a contrasting background, the fan design becomes the focal point of the same quilt with everyday fabrics.

SECTION 1A

Holiday Lap Quilt Instructions

Using a border print for the large diamond pieces in the center of the quilt gives the illusion of strip piecing. Cutting large shapes makes the quilt easy to assemble. You will be surprised at how quickly this quilt can be sewn and quilted. Consider making one or more for holiday gifts.

Finished Quilt Size: 58" x 75"
Block Size: 12"
Skill Level: Intermediate

Border prints are readily available to use in this type of design. If you wish to use other types of fabrics, you can strip piece to create a simulated border print.

❄ Materials

¾ yd. deer print (for fan blades)
1 yd. diamond tree print (for background diamonds)
2½ yd. snowflake print (for fan blades, background of fan blocks, binding and
    corner triangles)
3½ yd. snow border print (for center diamonds and borders)
3½ yd. silhouette print for backing
Template plastic
Permanent marker
62" x 78" piece of fusible batting
Coordinating threads for piecing and quilting
Rotary cutter and cutting mat

❄ Cutting Instructions

Cutting instructions are based on 40" wide fabrics. WOF = Width of Fabric

The patterns needed are the fan blade and diamond which include all seam allowances. From the full-size pattern trace the patterns onto the template plastic with a permanent marker, cut out and use these templates to cut the following pieces.

For the fans

Using the fan blade template, refer to the fan blade layout and cut the following:

(8) 12½" snowflake print squares
16 fan blades from the snowflake print
24 fan blades from the deer print

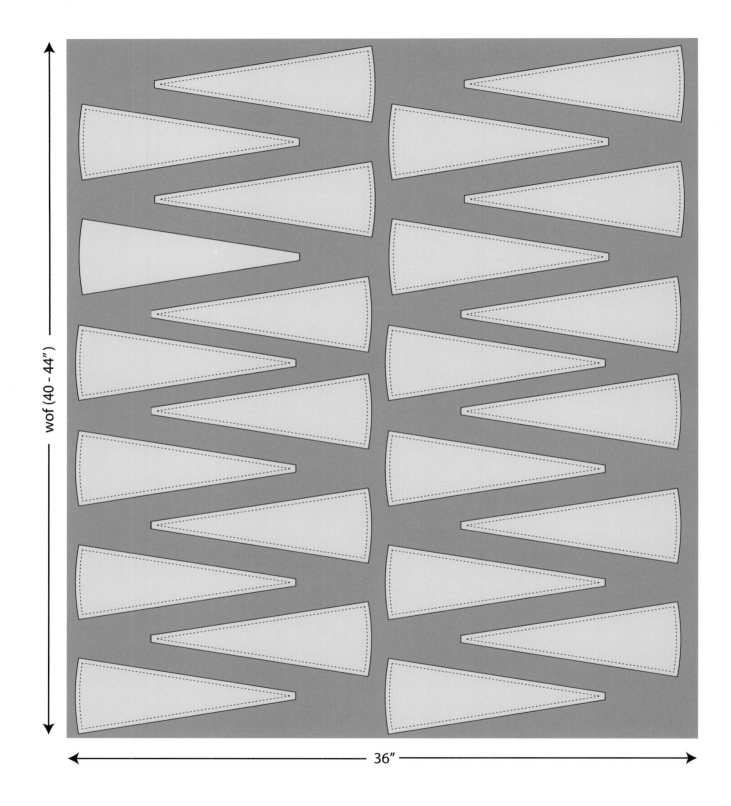

Optimize the use of your fabric by inverting your pattern to cut the fan blades.

For the star and background diamonds

Use the diamond template to cut the following pieces:

8 diamonds fussy cut from the snow border print
8 diamond shapes from the tree diamond print

Use a rotary cutter and ruler to quickly cut the large background diamonds for this project.

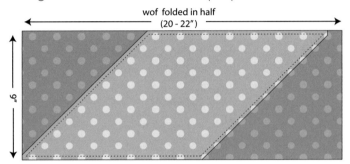

Using a border print for the large diamond pieces in the center of the quilt gives the illusion of strip piecing. Line up the pattern carefully to mark the pattern on exact repeats of the fabric. Mark all diamond pieces on the wrong side at the ¼" point indicated in the illustration.

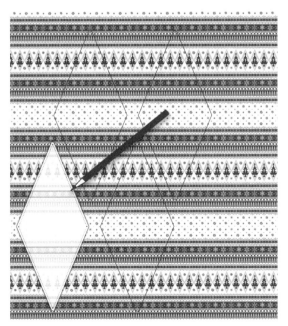

Fussy cut border print diamonds and mark start and stop points for sewing the diamonds.

For the corner setting triangles
(2) 17¾" squares from the snowflake print

For the border
(2) 8½" x 60" lengthwise strips of the snow border print

For the binding
(7) 2" x WOF strips snowflake print

❄ Sewing the Blocks

1 Referring to the photo below, sew two snowflake print fan blades together with three deer print fan blades.

Choosing the same fabric for the background and two blades blends the fan shape into the background, creating a snowflake effect.

2 Repeat to make a total of eight fans.

3 Turn under and press a ¼" seam allowance on the curved edge of the fan and position it on the 12½" snowflake background square. Pin in place and machine or hand appliqué the fan to the 12½" background square, basting the straight edges together.

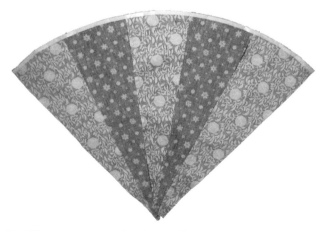

Fusible tapes can make the appliqué process easier, especially if you are stitching by machine.

As you can see, the backing tape is easy to remove. Even furry assistants can pitch in and help with this process.

You can use a ¼" Stitch Witchery fusible web or ¼" Wash Away Wonder Tape to secure the folded edge in place while you sew. The ¼" fusible web must be heat set in place at the edge of the fan, following the manufacturer's instructions. Take care to ease around the gentle curve. Fold in ¼" and fuse the seam allowance around the curve of the fan.

The water soluble tape must be clipped to ease the curve, then finger pressed in place. Position the tape around the curved edge of the fan and then remove the backing paper and finger press the ¼" seam allowance. The advantage to using the water-soluble tape is that it does not gum up your needle and will totally disappear when immersed in water, so there is no stiffness around the appliqué.

❄ Assembling the Quilt Top:

1 Assemble two star diamond pieces as per the illustration below, matching the stripes and leaving ¼" open at the beginning of each seam. Backstitch to secure. Repeat to make four sets.

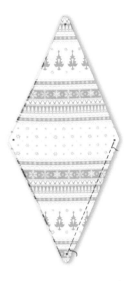

Start and stop sewing at the marked dots to prepare for insetting the fan blocks.

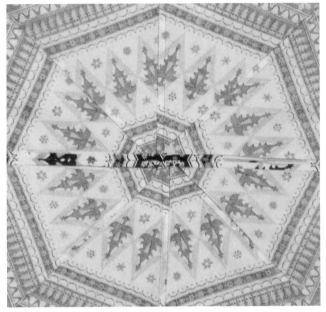

When so many seams come together in the center, it is wise to try and reduce the bulk by pressing the final joining seam open.

2 Sew two pairs together to create a half star, again leaving ¼" open at the beginning and end of the seam. Repeat to make the other half. Press seams in one direction.

3 Sew the two halves together to create the quilt center star and press that seam open to reduce bulk for adding the fan blocks.

Back of diamond with seams pressed in one direction.

You are now ready to begin insetting the fan blocks in your quilt center.

4 Referring to the diagram, inset one fan block in between two star points. Pin one edge of the fan block to the outside edge of the star and stitch from the ¼" starting mark on the diamond piece. Backstitch to secure and stitch to the end at the ¼" mark.

5 Lift the presser foot and remove the piece. Pivot the two pieces, arranging the two sides together for the next seam. Pin from the outside of the star to the inside of the fan block and stitch as before.

6 Continue working in this manner until you have set in all the fan blocks. Marking accurately and stitching carefully will help to make this technique easy to accomplish. Press all seams open for less bulk.

7 In the same manner, set in the outside diamond shapes, following the Quilt Top Layout on page 28.

8 Cut the large snowflake print squares in half diagonally.

9 Fold your corner triangles in half to find the center and pin to one side of the quilt top, matching the center point of one of the fan blocks. Stitch in place and add the other four snowflake corner triangles in the same manner. Refer to the Quilt Top Layout.

Fan Blade Inset Diagram

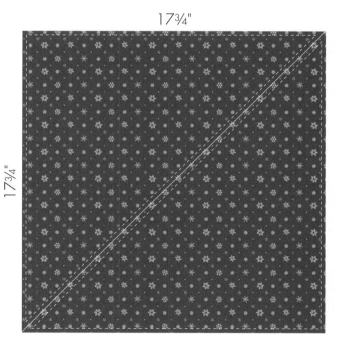

17¾"

17¾"

Cutting diagram

Assembling the large blocks and corner setting triangles is easy to master with careful pinning and marking of the diamond pieces.

❄ Borders & Finishing

1 Sew the 8½" x 60" snow stripe borders on the top and bottom of the quilt top. Press and trim any excess.

2 Layer your quilt backing, batting and quilt top, baste and quilt as desired. The quilt pictured on page 23 was quilted with echoed diamonds in the background diamonds and radiating lines following the fan blades. The border print areas were quilted around the geometric lines of the fabric pattern.

3 Trim and square the quilt and bind as desired with the 2" snowflake strips. See the basic instructions for binding suggestions.

Refer to the What Color is Your Holiday? section on page 123 for alternate color possibilities for all your holiday projects.

Everyday Lap Quilt Instructions

To achieve a very different look for every day, use two coordinating small prints for piecing the inner diamond star points instead of a border print and an additional print for the outside background diamonds. By featuring the fan shapes, a new design emerges from the same basic pattern pieces.

Finished Quilt Size: 58" x 75"
Block Size: 12"
Skill Level: Intermediate

Quilt Layout

Materials

¼ yd. small salmon dot print (for fan blades)

½ yd. brown dot print (for fan blades)

½ yd. brown mini floral print (for star)

½ yd. brown stripe (for binding)

¾ yd. dark brown and salmon circle print (for borders)

½ yd. tan stripe print (for fan blades)

1 yd. salmon arrow print (for background diamonds)

1¼ yd. brown and salmon vine print (for star and corner triangles)

1¼ yd. light tan print (for background of fan blocks)

3½ yd. for backing

62" x 78" piece of fusible batting

Template plastic

Marking tool for ¼" seam allowances

Permanent marker for tracing patterns

Threads for piecing and quilting

Rotary cutter and cutting mat

Always be sure to have someone test the comfort of any new quilt you make.

Cutting Instructions

Follow the detailed instructions in the Holiday version to cut and sew your fan and diamond pieces. Cutting instructions are based on 40"-wide fabric. WOF = Width of Fabric

For the fans

(8) 12½" squares from the light tan

8 fan blades from the salmon dot print

16 fan blades from each of the tan stripe print and the brown dot print

For the star and background diamonds

6 diamonds from the brown mini floral print and the brown vine print

12 diamonds from the salmon arrow print

For the corner setting triangles

(2) 17¾" squares from the brown vine print; subcut diagonally to make 4 triangles

For the border

(3) 8½" x WOF strips of the dark brown and salmon circle print

For the binding

(7) 2" x WOF strips from the brown stripe print

Sewing the Blocks

1 Referring to the diagrams on page 25, sew two brown dot, two tan stripe and one salmon dot fan blades together, using the quilt photograph on page 29 as a reference. Be sure to follow the suggested piecing sequence, with light fan blades on the outside of the block, which will contrast with the dark star diamonds when they are sewn together.

2 Repeat to make a total of eight fans.

3 Turn under and press a ¼" seam allowance on the curved edge of the fan and position it on the 12½" light tan background square. Pin in place and machine or hand appliqué the fan to the block.

Assembling the Quilt Top

1 Assemble two star diamond pieces as per the photograph, alternating the two brown colors and leaving ¼' open at the beginning of each seam. Backstitch to secure. Repeat to make four sets. Start and stop sewing at the marked dots to prepare for insetting the fan blocks.

2 Sew two pairs together to create a half star, again leaving the ¼" open at the beginning of the seam. Repeat to make the other half.

3 Sew the two halves together to create the quilt center star and press the seams open to reduce bulk for adding the fan blocks.

4 Referring to the photograph on page 29, inset one fan block in between two star points. Pin one edge of the fan block to the outside edge of the star and stitch from the ¼" starting mark on the diamond piece. Backstitch to secure and stitch to the end at the ¼" mark.

5 Lift the presser foot and remove the piece. Pivot the two pieces, arranging the two sides together for the next seam. Pin from the outside of the star to the inside of the fan block and stitch as before.

6 Continue working in this manner until you have set in all the fan blocks. Marking accurately and stitching carefully will help to make this technique easy to accomplish. Press all seams open for less bulk.

7 In the same manner, set in the outside salmon arrow diamond shapes.

8 Fold your brown vine corner triangles in half to find the center and pin to one side of the quilt top, matching the center point of one of the fan blocks. Stitch in place and add the other three brown vine corner triangles in the same manner. Refer to the Quilt Layout.

Borders & Finishing

1 Sew the 8½" x 60" brown circle borders on the top and bottom of the quilt. Press and trim any excess.

2 Layer the quilt backing, batting and quilt top, baste and quilt as desired. The diamonds in the quilt pictured were quilted with a continuous line design (provided in the pattern section) and radiating lines following the fan blades. The border print areas were quilted with an allover meandering design around the circles in the print.

3 Trim and square the quilt and bind as desired with the 2" brown stripe strips. See the Basic Quilting Lessons for binding suggestions.

Mantel Cover

Holiday

*Continue the elegant tone in decorating for the winter holidays
with this charming mantel cover. Create a warm, inviting look for your fireplace.
Make as many or as few panels as you need to custom fit your area.
Use this pattern to make a unique window valance, as well.*

SECTION 2A

Mantel Cover Instructions

Instructions for the every day Holiday and Window Valances pictured here can be found in the Bedroom Chapter, Section 4. Use the number of 10" flaps required to cover your window. You can overlap the flaps to adjust to in-between measurements for a custom fit.

Finished Size: 60" wide x 7" deep
½ Length from 9½" x 14½"

❄ Materials

⅔ yd. light blue tree diamond print

1¼ yd. deer print for backing of flaps

1¼ yd. dark blue snowflake print

7" x 60" piece of fusible batting

Three 12" x 18" sheets template plastic or
pattern paper

Permanent marker

❄ Cutting & Sewing Instructions

Cutting instructions are based on 40"-wide fabric. WOF=Width of Fabric

1 Trace all pattern pieces from pattern sheet
onto template plastic (or pattern paper)
with permanent marker for the four sizes of
flaps.

2 If using template plastic, cut out the pattern
pieces on the traced line. If using paper,
rough cut around the shapes.

3 Trace around the plastic pattern pieces
on the wrong side of the fabric, referring
to the cutting chart below. If using paper
patterns, layer your fabric, pin the pattern
in place and cut multiple pieces at the
same time.

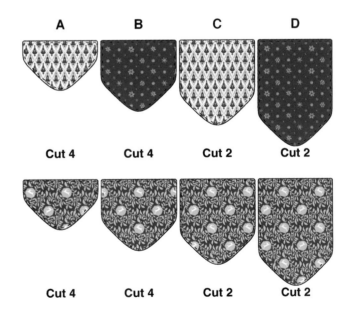

Cut 4 size A pieces from the blue tree diamond print and 4 from the deer print

Cut 4 size B pieces from the blue snowflake print and 4 from the deer print

Cut 2 size C pieces from the blue tree diamond print and 2 from the deer print

Cut 2 size D pieces from the blue snowflake print and 2 from the deer print

4 Place one of the size A blue tree diamond pieces right sides together on top of a size A deer print and stitch down one side, around the curve and up the other side, leaving the top open. Repeat to make four of these pieces.

5 Repeat the process using the size B, C, and D pieces.

6 Clip the curves and turn right side out. Press each piece. Refer to the diagram for suggestions on clipping the curves.

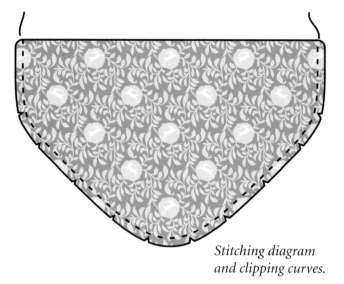

Stitching diagram and clipping curves.

7 Cut two 16" x WOF pieces of the blue snowflake print and stitch short ends together. Trim to measure 62".

Stitching the shelf piece.

8 Fold the shelf piece in half lengthwise with wrong sides together and press.

9 Open the folded piece and place the fusible batting next to the fold, centering on the piece and fuse in place according to manufacturer's directions. There will be 1" of extra fabric around the three edges, which will be trimmed after the quilting is finished.

Insert fusible batting.

10 Quilt as desired. The sample was quilted with an allover meandering design.

11 Mark 1" in around the outside edges with chalk and baste at the edge of the quilted portion. Trim the top layer about ¼" from the edge of the chalk or basting line, leaving the 1" of excess fabric in the backing at the sides and bottom.

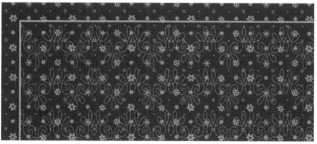

Quilting the shelf piece and marking the 1" edges.

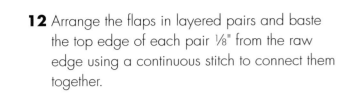

12 Arrange the flaps in layered pairs and baste the top edge of each pair ⅛" from the raw edge using a continuous stitch to connect them together.

13 Line up the layered mantel "flaps" on top of the quilted shelf fabric, right sides and raw edges of the quilted portion together, as shown, and pin in place. The excess fabric around the edges will be turned to form a self-binding after the flaps are stitched in place.

14 Stitch through all layers.

15 Fold and press the fabric edge ¼" on the back unfinished edge of the shelf fabric.

16 Turn in again ¼" and pin in place. Hand or machine stitch to secure.

17 Repeat this process to fold and stitch the side binding.

Layering flaps

Stitching flaps to shelf

Pinning self-binding

Self-binding sewn in place

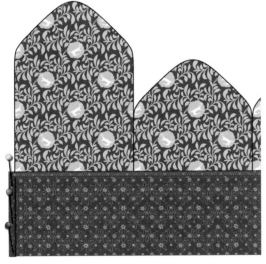

Finished edge

Folding self-edge

SECTION 3

Decorative & Organizational Accessories

Holiday   Everyday

Using some basic sewing techniques,
you can create some fun accessories for any room in your home.
Once you make one of these dimensional pieces, you can become
addicted to accessorizing, so beware.

SECTION 3A

Wall Sconce

Finished Size: 6" x 14"

Materials

Small ornaments in several colors will brighten up your holiday décor.

❄ Holiday Version

Fat quarter blue border stripe print

Fat quarter blue deer print

ꙮ Everyday Version

Fat quarter brown mini floral print

Fat quarter salmon dot prints

Both Versions

(2) 12" x 20" pieces Timtex

(4) 12" x 20" pieces paper-backed
    fusible web

13" square fusible batting

Template plastic

Thread to coordinate

Permanent marker to coordinate (optional)

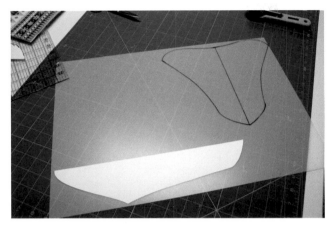

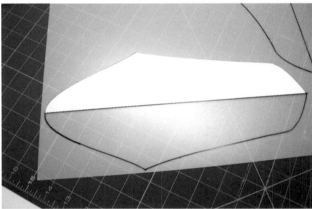

Patterns are easy to trace and cut with sharp scissors.

❄ Directions

1 Trace all pattern pieces from the pattern sheet onto template plastic (or pattern paper) with permanent marker for the two pattern pieces. By using template plastic for your patterns, you will be able to make multiple sconces to complement your décor. Always use a permanent marker on the plastic and mark your pattern pieces for future use.

Teflon pressing sheets are handy to keep near your iron and pressing surface when working with fusibles.

2 Fuse the fat quarters of fabric onto both sides of the Timtex, using the fusible web, according to manufacturer's instructions.

3 Mark the pattern pieces on the interfaced fabric and cut out carefully with scissors.

Using a Teflon pressing sheet will help you to keep your iron and ironing surface clean. We suggest using one below your fusible work and one on top, between your work and iron. They are easy to clean by simply rubbing the fusible from the surface, if any of the fusible product is transferred in the fusing process.

4 Satin stitch around any edges that will not be sewn together to finish the edges.

5 Position the pocket sconce piece on the background piece and pin in place.

6 Stitch around all the outside edges with a zigzag stitch to baste in position.

7 Set your machine for a wide zigzag stitch with a small stitch length and satin stitch around all the edges. Test on a scrap to determine the correct settings.

Use the smaller sconce patterns to create ornaments similar to the Victorian cone ornaments, which you can fill with holiday flowers or small gifts. You can also use these in a wall arrangement with the larger sconces.

8 Complete the piece by stitching a buttonhole in the top center of the background piece and thread a coordinating ribbon or cord through the hole. Tie a knot and use that to hang your sconce on the wall. You can also hang the sconce on a hook or nail directly through the buttonhole, without a hanging cord.

An alternative to using a satin stitch is to couch a decorative cording or yarn on these outside edges. Use an invisible thread in both the top and bobbin of your sewing machine. Set the zigzag stitch width at a wide setting and use a medium-length stitch. Hold the cording or yarn right up against the edge of the fused piece and carefully follow around the outside edge.

"Couching" the cord to the edge.

*Make permanent patterns in template plastic to use over again
to make new pieces for different seasons and different uses. You will find uses
for one of these bowls in every room of your house to organize your
desk accessories and display your collections.*

SECTION 3B

Holiday Potpourri or Candy Bowl

Finished Size: 5½" wide x 4" high

Materials

❆ Holiday Version

13" square blue tree diamond print
13" square blue snowflake print

ℚ Everyday Version

13" chocolate vine print
13' salmon dot print

Both Versions

13" square Timtex
Two 13" squares paper-backed fusible web
13" square of template plastic
Thread to coordinate
Permanent marker to coordinate (optional)
Chopstick or skewer to score the interfaced
    pieces

❄ Directions

1 Trace the pattern from the pattern sheet onto the template plastic with permanent marker. Cut out on the drawn line.

2 Fuse the 13" squares of fabric onto both sides of the Timtex, using the fusible web, according to manufacturer's instructions.

3 Center the pattern and trace around the outside edges on the lighter fabric with permanent marker.

4 Carefully cut out on the drawn line.

5 Color the white edges with a coordinating permanent marker, if desired. These edges will be satin stitched, and some white may show through if your stitches are not close enough together. Coloring the edges will camouflage any open areas of stitching.

6 Using your pattern as a reference, score the straight lines in the center to create a square base.

7 Fold up two of the adjacent sides and pin to hold together.

8 Set your machine to sew a satin stitch with a long width and a very short length, with stitches close together. Test on a scrap to determine the correct settings.

9 Choose a coordinating or contrasting thread for both the top and bobbin and begin stitching around the top edges. If you have not colored the edges prior to the stitching, you may see some exposed white areas. Either stitch over these areas again, or use the colored permanent marker at this point to cover the exposed white edge.

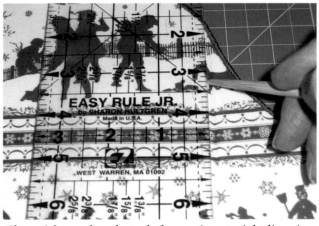

Chopsticks are handy tools for scoring straight lines in the areas to be folded. Scoring tools are also available in your local craft and hobby stores in the scrapbooking section.

10 Repeat to close the other three sides. The interfacing is very forgiving and can be bent or folded to fit under the sewing machine. You can press when finished if wrinkles remain in the finished piece.

Use as a table top waste basket in your office or a thread and scrap catcher in your sewing room. This size makes a wonderful holiday decoration in your family room, holding winter potpourri or candy. Consider using pine cones and silk flowers as a holiday display. The everyday version is shown below.

You will find many uses around the house for this small container.
It will be handy to hold remote controls by the television or as a receptacle by your door
as a place to leave your iPod or cell phone. Eliminate the need to search for your
elusive keys by depositing them as soon as you come in the door.

SECTION 3C

Cell Phone/PDA/Remote/iPod Holder

Finished Size: 5½" wide x 3" deep x 2" high

Materials

❄ Holiday Version

9" x 12" piece blue deer print
9" x 12" piece blue snowflake print

☯ Everyday Version

9" x 12" piece brown stripe
9" x 12" piece salmon vine print

Both Versions

9" x 12" piece Timtex
(2) 9" x 12" pieces of paper-backed fusible web
9" x 12" piece of template plastic or cardboard
Thread to coordinate
Permanent marker to coordinate (optional)

❄ Directions

1 Trace the patterns from the pattern sheet onto the template plastic with permanent marker. Cut out on the drawn line.

2 Fuse the 9" x 12" rectangle of fabric onto both sides of the Timtex, using the fusible web, according to manufacturer's instructions.

3 Center the pattern and trace around the outside edges on the lighter fabric with permanent marker.

4 Carefully cut out on the drawn line.

5 Color the white edges with a coordinating permanent marker, if desired. These edges will be satin stitched and some white may show through if your stitches are not close enough together. Coloring the edges will camouflage any open areas of stitching.

6 Using your pattern as a reference, score the straight lines in the center to create a rectangular base.

7 Fold up two of the adjacent sides and pin to hold together.

8 Set your machine to sew a satin stitch with a long width and a very short length, with stitches close together. Test on a scrap to determine the correct settings. Begin sewing at the top edge and stitch to the bottom folded edge.

9 Choose a coordinating or contrasting thread for both the top and bobbin and begin stitching around the top edges. If you have not colored the edges prior to the stitching, you may see some exposed white areas. Either stitch over these areas again, or use the colored permanent marker at this point to cover the exposed white edge.

10 Repeat to close the other three sides. The interfacing is very forgiving and can be bent or folded to fit under the sewing machine. Press with an iron if necessary.

Everyday versions of the potpourri and cell phone holder.

Use as a place to gather keys and pocket change in the foyer or business cards on a desk. Use in your family room to hold remote, PDA, iPod or phone.

Keep one of these handy by your desk to hold unpaid bills, photos or correspondence.
Use several during the holidays to hold your greeting cards.
This will also be handy in the foyer to deposit outgoing
or incoming mail for other family members.

SECTION 3D

Card Display

Finished Size: 9" wide x 10½' high

Materials (for each card holder)

❄ Holiday Version

Fat quarter blue tree diamond print
Fat quarter blue snowflake print

☯ Everyday Version

Fat quarter brown circles print
Fat quarter square salmon arrows print

Both Versions

18" x 22" piece Timtex
18" x 22" piece paper-backed
    fusible web
Template plastic or cardboard
Thread to coordinate
Permanent marker to coordinate (optional)

❄ Directions

1 Trace the patterns from the pattern sheet onto the template plastic with permanent marker. Cut out on the drawn line.

2 Fuse the fat quarters of fabric onto both sides of the Timtex, using the fusible web, according to manufacturer's instructions.

3 Mark the pattern pieces on the interfaced fabric and cut out carefully with scissors.

4 Satin stitch around all outside edges. An alternative to finishing the edges is to couch a decorative cording or yarn on these edges. See page 40 for a photo of the couching technique.

Use all types of cording or decorative trim to finish the edges of your dimensional pieces.

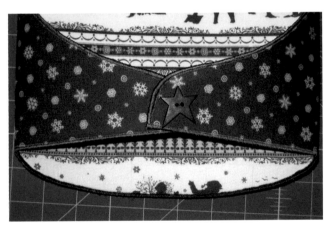

Finish all edges with satin stitching.

An alternative to finishing the edges is to couch a decorative cording or yarn on these edges.

5 Referring to the pattern for placement, score the straight lines where the card holder will be folded, using a chopstick or scoring tool from the craft shop.

6 Fold the sides in, overlapping the ends by approximately 1". Pin in place and stitch in position. Set your machine for a wide zigzag stitch with a zero stitch length. If you wish to secure with a button, hand stitch in place.

There are many different types of decorative buttons that would be fun to use on your card holder. The everyday version features a butterfly button where the card holder is stitched closed and uses a round button to secure the hanger.

7 Fold the bottom edge up inside the sides and stitch 1" along the bottom edge from the outside edges. This will secure the bottom edge so that your cards will be held securely.

8 Complete the piece by stitching a button in the top center of the background piece, with a hang cord stitched on the back at the same time.

You can create a hang cord by cutting a strip of fabric 1¼" x 6". Fold both outside long edges in to the center and press. Fold the strip in half and stitch along the length. Use this cord to hang your card displays individually.

You can sew the hanger to the back of the card holder when you stitch on your decorative button. Or, you can hand stitch a plastic ring to the back for hanging on a hook or nail. These are available in your sewing or craft stores.

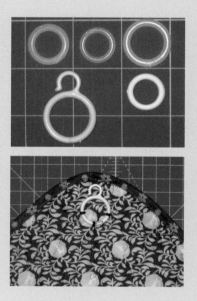

Glue or stitch magnetic strips (available in your local office supply or craft store) to the back of your card display to hang on your refrigerator. Keep your coupons, shopping and to-do lists handy.

Keep one of these handy by your desk to hold unpaid bills, photos or correspondence.
Use several during the holidays to hold your greeting cards.
This will also be handy in the foyer to deposit outgoing
or incoming mail for other family members.

SECTION 3E

Multiple Card Display and Quilt

Materials (in addition to the card display units on pages 45-47)

❄ Quilted Wall Hanging

1 yd. blue deer print
⅛ yd. blue snowflake print for binding
16" x 42" piece batting
Plastic rings
Coordinating thread for quilting

❄ Instructions

1 Make three card displays from page 45 and set aside.

2 Cut two pieces of fabric 12" x WOF.

3 Layer the backing, batting and quilt front and baste. Quilt as desired. The quilt pictured was quilted with an allover star and loop pattern.

4 Trim the piece to measure 11" x 24". Use the template for the mantel cover on the pattern sheet to trim the top of the piece in a curved shape.

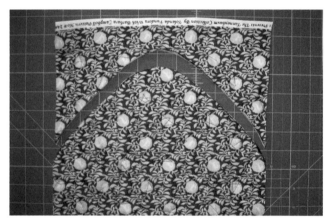

5 Cut two 2" x WOF strips from the snowflake print and use to bind the quilt.

6 Hand sew two plastic rings on the back of the quilt for hanging.

7 Instead of making hanging cords for your card holders, use decorative buttons and stitch to the quilt through the buttonholes. Refer to the photo of the finished piece for placement of the card holders on the quilt.

If desired, you can make only two of the card holders and shorten the quilt by approximately 12".

Multiple Card Display and Quilt | 49

Jumping Jacks

Holiday

Everyday

Fun for young and old alike, these timeless toys are easy to assemble and fun to make. Once you finish your first, you'll be inspired to make more for gifts. Everyone will love these adorable toys. The patterns can be reduced to ornament size, if you wish.

SECTION 4A

Jumping Santa

Finished Size: 16"

Jolly doesn't begin to describe how Santa looks as he jumps and dances around.

Using a variety of fabric prints can give your Jumping Jacks a very different appearance.

❄ Materials (Makes one Jumping Santa)

Fat eighth (9" x 22") red snowflake fabric

Fat eighth (9" x 22") red snow stripe fabric

3" square of flesh colored fabric

4" x 3" piece of white fleece or felt

2 sheets 8½" x 11" template plastic or cardstock

Permanent marker

1 - 2 yd. fusible web (depending on the width; must have at least four 9" x 22" pieces)

Teflon pressing sheet or parchment paper

1 yd. Timtex or other sturdy interfacing

(6) ½" two-holed buttons for joints

2 decorative buttons for belt and hat

½" red pompom for nose

Fabric glue

Permanent fabric markers

2 yd. of ⅛" cording for pull strings

Bead for handle

Hammer and thick nail

❄ Directions

1 Trace around all pattern pieces from the pattern sheet onto template plastic or cardboard with permanent marker for Jumping Santa. If you prefer to scan and print directly on cardstock, see sidebar.

2 Fuse the paper-backed interfacing to the wrong side of the red snowflake and red stripe fabrics.

3 Fuse the red snowflake fabric to one side of the interfacing and the red stripe fabric to the back.

You can scan the pattern pieces from the book and print directly on cardstock if your printer will feed heavyweight paper or cardstock. Check your printer manual.

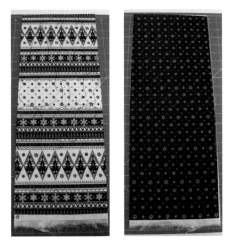

Fusing fabric to front and back of interfacing

4 Trace around the pattern pieces except for the mustache and beard on the stripe side of the fabric, referring to the photo for placement (especially for the belt, cuffs and hat brim). The rest of the body will feature the red snowflake on the front, so is not as fussy. Cut the pattern pieces on the drawn line.

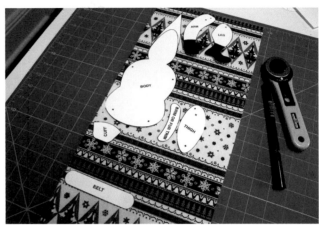

Positioning the pattern pieces

5 Using a lightbox or window, trace the beard and mustache pieces onto cardstock. Place your traced pattern face down, top with a piece of 4" x 3" piece fusible web and 4" x 3" piece of white fleece. Fuse the fleece to the cardstock from the fabric side.

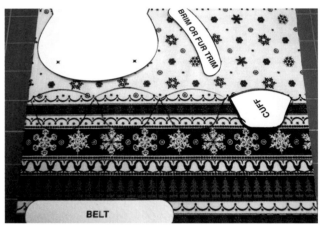

Fussy cutting some of the pieces

6 Cut out the beard and mustache pieces.

7 Use a light box to trace the face pattern onto cardstock, including facial details.

Fussy cut pieces

8 Fuse the flesh colored fabric onto the front of the cardstock face. Use the lines showing through to "paint" the features with permanent fabric markers. Fuse the face in place on the body. Glue or fuse the face to the front of your Santa, referring to the photo for placement.

9 If desired, use permanent fabric markers to color the white edges of the body, hat, arm and leg pieces. This is recommended when the color of the fabric pieces is dark and the contrast between the white interfacing is very noticeable.

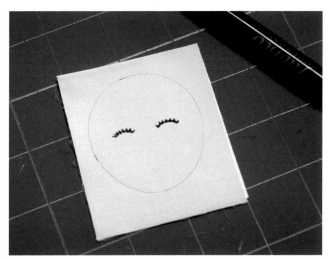

Marking the facial features through the fabric

Fusing Santa's face using a protective Teflon ironing sheet

10 Use the dot on the arm and thigh pattern pieces as a reference to where holes need to be punched to thread the pull strings. We recommend using a hammer and nail to punch through the pieces where marked. Be sure to use a scrap of wood behind your pattern pieces to avoid damaging your work surface.

Make holes to insert cording for final assembly steps.

It might be necessary to punch through from both sides to get a clean hole.

Check to make sure you have a hole that your cording will pass through.

11 Referring to the diagrams of the layout, assemble the arm pieces, the leg pieces and body.

12 It is very important to sew a ½" two-holed button in between the two pieces where the arms join to the body, the knee joins the upper leg and the leg joins the body. This will give your jumping jack a looser motion. Refer to diagrams for placement and mark the body, arms and legs where they will join.

13 Starting with the upper body, sew a button on the back where one of the arms will join, using a zigzag width that will fit in the buttonholes. Set your stitch length at zero to stitch in place.

14 Place the body front-side up and position the arm in place, matching up the points where they should join. Use the stitches from the button as a guide to position your needle in the correct position. Manually test to make sure your piece is lined up correctly and then stitch over the existing stitches to secure the arm to the body.

15 Repeat this procedure to attach the lower leg to the thigh and the thigh to the body, making sure to first sew the button onto the piece that will be in the back. That would mean the back of the body where arms and legs join and the back of the lower leg.

16 Continue the assembly of the body parts in this manner until you have all the arm and leg pieces attached to the body.

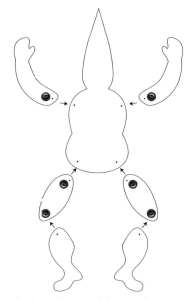

Assembly showing position of buttons on arm and thigh.

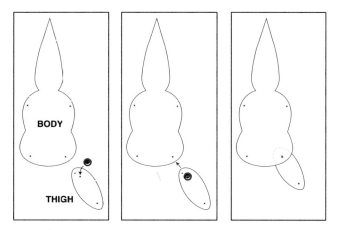

Sew button to thigh piece, then place in position behind Santa's body and line up to stitch through the buttonholes.

Correct assembly positions for arms and legs.

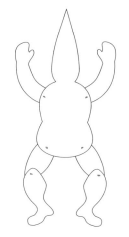

Insert one piece of cording through both arms.

Tie a knot close to the hole in the arm, leaving a 3" piece between the arms.

Secure the knot with fabric glue.

17 Finally, attach the hat brim, cuffs and belt. At this point you can sew on the decorative buttons (also with the same zigzag stitch). Leave the beard, nose and mustache until the end.

18 To create the movement, cut two pieces of cord measuring approximately 7" to connect the arms and legs. Using a large-eye needle, thread the cording through the connecting point of the left arm (indicated by the dot on the pattern) and then through the connecting point of the right arm. Tie a knot at each end, leaving a loop measuring approximately 3". Use fabric glue at the ends and on the knots of the cording to prevent it from unraveling. Repeat to connect the top of the legs where indicated on the pattern.

In lieu of a large-eye needle, you can wrap the cording with a piece of tape at the point where you will cut it to prevent unraveling while working with this cord. Snip the tape on an angle to create a "needle," which is helpful in threading the cord through the holes.

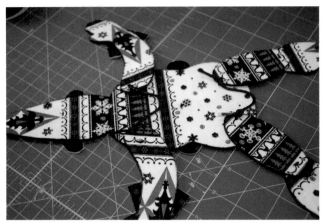

Check Santa's arm motion.

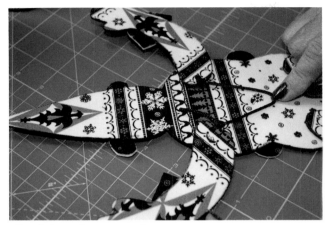

Cording in place for arms and legs.

19 Cut a piece of cording measuring 18" long and tie to the center of the arm loop. Bring the cording down and tie on a large bead. Bring the end of the cording back to the center of the leg loop and tie off.

20 Glue beard, nose and mustache in place to complete your Jumping Santa.

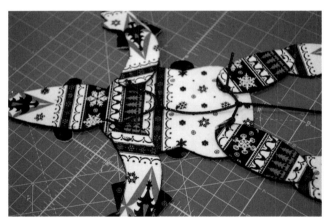

How to attach the pull cord.

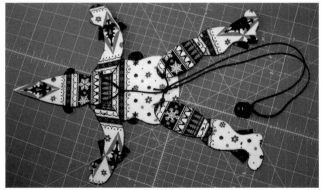

Pull cord with bead attached.

Santa with beard, nose and mustache in place.

21 Attach a 7" piece of cording to the top of the head and tie into a hanging loop. Use this loop to hang your Jumping Jack as a wall decoration or to hold in one hand while you pull his beaded handle to animate him. We secured the top tie while stitching on the decorative button to his hat. You could also hand or machine stitch the cord in place without the button.

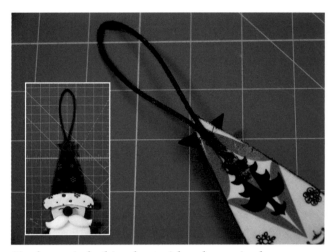

Top loop stitched in place with a decorative button.

If you prefer to make these Jumping Jack characters as ornaments, reduce the pattern pieces by 50% and do not animate them. Simply stitch together at the joints, eliminating the button and cording steps. We suggest you stitch the arms and legs in jumping poses to animate all your ornaments in different positions.

Mini jacks as ornaments.

Jumping Clown

Young and old alike are fascinated by these fun toys.

Finished Size: Clown 14"

❄ Materials
(Makes one Jumping Clown)

Fat quarter multicolored print

8" square green print

3" square of flesh colored fabric

3" x 4" piece red felt for hair

2" square pink felt or fleece for flower trim

2 sheets 8½" x 11" template plastic or cardstock

Permanent marker

1 - 2 yd. fusible web (depending on the width; must have at least four 9" x 22" pieces)

Teflon pressing sheet (optional)

1 yd. Timtex or other sturdy interfacing

(6) ½" two-holed buttons for joints

4 decorative buttons for belly and nose

Fabric glue (optional)

Permanent fabric markers

2 yd. ⅓" cording for pull strings

Bead for handle

❄ Directions

1 Follow the basic instructions and illustrations for making patterns, cutting and sewing the Jumping Santa to construct your Jumping Clown.

2 Fuse the paper-backed interfacing to the wrong side of the multicolored fabric and the green fabric.

3 Fuse the multicolored fabric to one side of the interfacing and the green print fabric to the other side.

4 Trace around the pattern pieces on the multicolored and green fabric, except for the hair, flower and face. Cut the pattern pieces on the drawn line.

5 Place your hair pattern on the 3" x 4" piece red felt. Pin in place and cut carefully around the pattern.

6 Use the same method above to cut out a flower from the pink felt or fleece.

7 Use a light box to trace the face pattern onto cardstock.

8 Fuse the flesh colored fabric onto the front of the cardstock face. Use the lines showing through to "paint" the features with permanent fabric markers. Glue the face to the front of your clown, referring to the photo for placement.

9 If desired, use permanent fabric markers to color the white edges of the body, hat, arm and leg pieces. This is recommended when the color of the fabric pieces is dark and the contrast between the white interfacing is very noticeable.

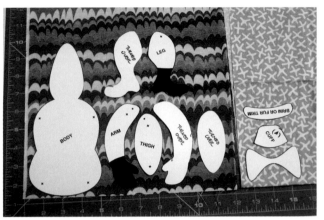

Pattern pieces.

Clown's hair.

Clown face.

10 Refer to the instructions and illustrations on page 54 in the Jumping Santa section, Step 10 to attach the pull strings to the body.

11 Referring to the photo of the finished Clown Jumping Jack, lay the arm pieces, the leg pieces and body in position.

12 It is very important to sew a ½" two-holed button in between the two pieces where the arms join to the body, the knee joins the upper leg and the leg joins the body. This will give your jumping jack a looser motion. Refer to diagrams on page 55 for placement and mark the body, arms and legs where they will join.

13 Starting with the upper body, sew a button on the back where one of the arms will join, using a zigzag width that will fit in the buttonholes. Set your stitch length at zero to stitch in place.

14 Place the body front side up and position the arm in place, matching up the points where they should join. Use the stitches from the button as a guide to position your needle in the correct position. Manually test to make sure your piece is lined up correctly and then stitch over the existing stitches to secure the arm to the body.

15 Repeat this procedure to attach the lower leg to the thigh and the thigh to the body, making sure to first sew the button onto the piece that will be in the back. That would mean the back of the body where arms and legs join and the back of the lower leg.

16 Continue the assembly of the body parts in this manner until you have all the arm and leg pieces attached to the body.

17 Finally, attach the hat brim, cuffs and bow tie. At this point you can sew on the decorative buttons (also with the same zigzag stitch). You can either stitch or glue the decorative flower onto the clown's bow tie.

18 To create the movement, cut two pieces of cord measuring approximately 7" to connect the arms and legs. Using a large-eye needle, thread the cording through the connecting point of the left arm (indicated by the dot on the pattern) and then through the connecting point of the right arm. Tie a knot at each end, leaving a loop measuring approximately 3". Use fabric glue at the ends and on the knots of the cording to prevent it from unraveling.

19 Cut a piece of cording measuring 18" long and tie to the center of the arm loop. Bring the cording down and tie on a large bead. Bring the end of the cording back to the center of the leg loop and tie off.

20 Attach a 7" piece of cording to the top of the head and tie into a hanging loop. Attach this loop to hang your Jumping Jack as a wall decoration or to hold in one hand while you pull his beaded handle to animate him.

Reversible Tabletop Tree Skirt/Table Cover

Holiday

Everyday

This tree skirt has been designed to double as a table cover,
so there is no hole cut for the trunk of the tree. Simply set the tree in its stand on top
of the skirt and wrap a little leftover stripe or snowflake fabric around the tree stand.
The blue version can also serve as a table cover for Chanukah.
Use a commercial border print as we did in the holiday version
or create your own border print by strip-piecing fabric strips in the everyday version.

SECTION 5A

Holiday Tabletop Tree Skirt

The size of this tree skirt is perfect for a tabletop display. It has also been designed as a reversible table cover to extend its use throughout the winter season.

Size: 43" diameter
Skill Level: Beginner

This quilt can be assembled with a "pillowcase" method instead of the traditional layering, quilting and binding. Refer to the Basic Quilting Lessons for this technique.

❄ Materials

1 ¼ yd. blue deer print for triangles
1 ¼ yd. blue tree diamond print for triangles
1 ⅜ yd. blue snowflake print for trapezoid borders and binding

2 yd. blue silhouette stripe fabric for triangles
46" square piece of lightweight batting
Large pad of newsprint paper
Threads for piecing and quilting
Rotary cutter and cutting mat

❄ Cutting and Sewing Instructions

1 Using the pattern on the pattern sheet, make a paper template of your tree skirt triangle. Also make a template of the trapezoid border piece. Lay the paper template on top of the fabric and use your ruler and a permanent marker to draw the shape, which includes ¼" seam allowances.

2 Cut eight identical triangles from the blue silhouette print.

3 Cut four triangles from the blue deer print and four from the blue tree diamond print.

4 Cut eight 3¼" x WOF strips from the blue snowflake fabric. Fold each strip in half and then in half again across the width. Place the template with the marked side on the fold. Line up your ruler along the edge of the angle and cut. You will be cutting two trapezoids at a time with this method.

Cutting diagram for the silhouette print.

Cut trapezoids from a folded strip

There is an easy method to cut the triangles from the solid fabrics (where prints do not have to be matched as in the silhouette print). Follow the steps in the photos to tape your triangle template on the back of your ruler. Cut a 20" x WOF strip of your selected fabric. Fold one selvage side of the fabric toward the center. Place the ruler on the folded fabric, lining up the edge marked fold on the folded edge of the fabric and the bottom of the template on the cut edge. Use your rotary cutter to cut the angled side of the triangle. You will have enough fabric to cut two triangles from each 20" strip.

Ruler cutting method for triangles.

5 Cut four 2" x WOF strips for the binding.

6 Sew the large trapezoid border pieces to the bottom of all the triangles.

7 Sew the silhouette triangles together to create one side of the octagonal tree skirt.

8 Repeat this process, alternately sewing the blue deer print triangles and the blue tree diamond triangles for the other side.

9 Lay one of the octagonal quilt pieces on the batting and trim the batting to the same size and shape.

10 Layer the backing, batting and top and quilt as desired. The quilt pictured was quilted around the silhouette stripes from the front.

11 Bind with four 2" strips of the blue snowflake print, following directions in the Basic Instruction Section for mitering corners.

Sew the trapezoids to the triangles.

If you wish to make this a true tree skirt, after the quilting is finished, slit one of the seams apart to the center. Cut a circle of appropriately 5" from the center and bind around the outside edges, up one side of the slit, around the curve and down the other side of the slit. If you decide to do this, you will need to cut your binding on the bias to negotiate the curve. Increase the binding yardage accordingly. For this method, you will need about ⅞ yd. of fabric and need to cut and make approximately 220" of 2" bias binding.

Front and back of quilt showing two very different looks.

Using the same basic sewing techniques, you can sew strips of fabric together to create your own border print for a striking table cover that will be enjoyed year-round. Create matching reversible napkins to complete the coordinated look.

SECTION 5B

Everyday Reversible Table Topper

Finished Size: 43" diameter
Skill Level: Beginner

Materials

⅓ yd. salmon print (for binding)

⅔ yd. tan print

1 yd. dark brown and salmon
　　circle print

1 yd. salmon stripe

1¼ yd. dark brown vine print

1¼ yd. salmon vine print

1¾ yd. medium brown print

46" square piece of lightweight batting

Large pad of newsprint paper

Threads for piecing and quilting

Rotary cutter and cutting mat

If you prefer to have solid fabrics instead of the pieced triangles, change the yardage to 1¼ yd. each of two coordinating prints and cut as we did on the reverse side of this sample.

❄ Cutting Instructions

To create a unique border print for the front, cut:

Medium brown
(2) 2½" x WOF strips

Light tan
(4) 2½" x WOF strips

Salmon stripe
(4) 3½" x WOF strips

Dark brown and salmon circle print
(4) 3¾" x WOF strips

Medium brown print
(8) 3¼" strips; subcut into (16) 3¼" x 18¼" trapezoids (two trapezoids from each strip) for both the front and back borders

For the backing, cut:

Salmon vine print
(4) triangles

Dark brown vine print
(4) triangles

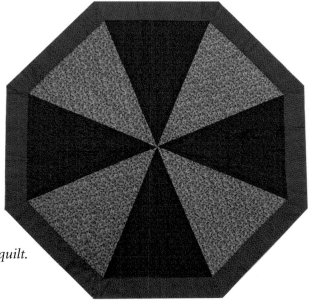

Back of everyday quilt.

❄ Sewing Instructions

1 To create the unique border print fabric, sew together the strips in the following order, referring to the illustration.

Dark brown and salmon, 3¾" strip
Salmon stripe, 3½" strip
Light tan, 2½" strip
Medium brown, 2½" strip
Light tan, 2½" strip
Salmon stripe, 3½" strip
Dark brown and salmon, 3¾" strip

The resulting strip set should measure 19½". Press all seams in one direction.

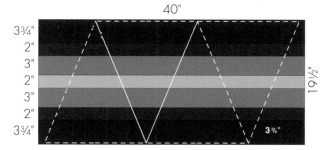

Strip set and cutting layout for triangles

2 Refer to the illustration above, cut the triangles from this strip set. Follow the instructions for the Holiday Tree Skirt to assemble your Reversible Table Topper.

Looks like the perfect size for a bistro set outdoors.

Instructions for making these reversible napkins can be found on page 77 in the Dining Room chapter.

The Dining Room

Striking red accessories against a dark green tablecloth
create a traditional look for your holiday entertaining.
We have supplied easy to modify pattern pieces for the place mats
and table runners which allow you to customize the size of your table settings.

Tablecloth

Holiday

Everyday

Reversible tablecloths can be made of coordinating or contrasting fabrics on either side to extend the life of your dining room ensembles. You can choose to piece both sides in fabrics for different seasons or make one side a solid backing for a less formal look.

SECTION 1A

Winter Holiday Tablecloth

A winter border print accents the edge of your table. Feature a holiday motif in the corner squares, or leave them plain. Done in the traditional holiday red and green, this tablecloth will create a festive look for your holiday meals.

Finished Tablecloth Size: 68" x 90"
Skill Level: Beginner

If you use different colorways for the front and back of the tablecloth, you may not wish to use a binding to secure top and bottom layers. Sew the top and bottom sections right sides together, leaving a 6" opening on one side. Turn to the right side, fold in the seam allowance in the opening and pin. Edge stitch around all four sides, which will close the opening and stabilize the tablecloth.

❄ Materials

¾ yd. red tree motif print (enough for four oval trees to appliqué in the corners)
1 yd. green reindeer print (for corner squares)
2 yd. green snowflake print
3 yd. green snowstripe border print
5¾ yd. red snowflake print (for backing and binding)
Paper-backed fusible web
Coordinating thread

❄ Cutting Instructions

From the red snowflake print

(8) 2" x WOF strips (for binding)

Cut 8

From the snowflake border print

(2) 14½" x 62½" lengthwise strips
and (2) 14½" x 40½" lengthwise strips
(for borders)

Cut 2

Cut 2

Other border prints are readily available to use in this type of design. If you wish to use a different border, calculate the width of the selected border design and adjust them to fit your table. If you wish to increase the overall size of the tablecloth and you are using 40" - 42" wide cotton, you may have to piece the center section.

If you use the fabric featured here, you will have small ovals left from cutting the corner tree motifs. Use these with fusible web and Timtex interfacing to create double-sided ornaments or napkin rings.

From the green reindeer print

(4) 15" squares

Cut 4

From the green snowflake print

(1) 40½" x 62½" piece (for center)

From the red snowflake print

cut and piece to measure 68½" x 90½" for the backing

❄ Sewing Instructions

1 Rough cut four oval tree motifs (or other large motif of your choice), leaving at least ½" around all outside edges. Fuse the paper-backed web to the wrong side of the trees, following the manufacturer's directions.

2 Carefully cut around the appliqué shape with a sharp scissors and remove the paper backing.

3 Fold the 15" squares on the diagonal both ways to determine the center of the block.

4 Remove the paper, center the tree motif diagonally on the square, and fuse in place, following manufacturer's directions.

5 Use a small zigzag or buttonhole stitch around the outside edge of the motif.

6 Trim the square to 14½", keeping the motif centered.

7 Sew a 14½" x 62½" green snowstripe border piece to the sides of the green snowflake print rectangle, making sure you orient the stripe print in the correct direction. Refer to the photograph.

8 Stitch the 14½" appliquéd squares to the ends of the remaining stripe prints, again referring to the photo for the direction of the appliquéd trees. Sew these pieced strips to the top and bottom. Press and trim evenly. See the photo on page 71.

9 Mark the centers of all sides of top and back of tablecloth.

10 Place both sides of the tablecloth, wrong sides together and pin around the edges to secure, matching up the centers and corners.

Fussy cut motif for corner squares of the tablecloth.

Center the motif diagonally on each corner square.

11 Sew the 2' x 42" red snowflake strips short ends together to make one long binding strip. Press seams open and press in half lengthwise.

12 Sew the raw edges of the binding to the pinned tablecloth on the wrong side, referring to the general instructions for applying binding in the Basic Quilting Lessons.

13 Turn the binding to the front side of the tablecloth folding the binding over to just cover the former stitching line and machine stitch in place using a small zigzag stitch.

*In order to increase the versatility in the dining room ensemble,
we have provided instructions for sewing a double-sided tablecloth.
One side is pieced with a striking border and the reverse side is plain.
Use your coordinating table runner, napkins, hot pads
and place mats to decorate either side.*

SECTION 1B

Everyday Tablecloth Instructions

Finished Tablecloth Size: 68" x 90"
Skill Level: Beginner

❄ Materials

½ yd. light brown print (for binding)
2 yd. salmon mini floral print
2 yd. brown circle print
3 yd. brown stripe
5¼ yd. salmon splinter print (for backing)
Coordinating thread

❄ Cutting Instructions

From the light brown print
(8) 2" x WOF strips (for binding)

From the brown circle print
(4) 14½" squares

From the salmon mini floral print
(1) 40½" x 62½" piece (for center)

From the brown stripe print
(2) 14½" x 62½" lengthwise strips
(2) 14½" x 40½" lengthwise strips
(for borders)

From the salmon splinter print
cut and piece the tablecloth back to measure 68½" x 90½"

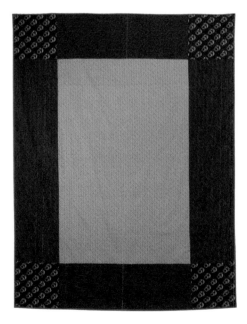

❄ Sewing Instructions

1 Sew a 14½" x 62½" brown stripe piece to the sides of the salmon mini floral print. Stitch the 14½" brown circle squares to the ends of the remaining stripe prints. Sew these pieced strips to the top and bottom. Press and trim evenly. See the tablecloth photograph.

2 Mark the centers of all sides of top and back of tablecloth.

3 Place both sides of the tablecloth, wrong sides together and pin around the edges to secure, matching up the centers and corners.

4 Sew the 2" x 42" light brown strips, short ends together to make one long binding strip. Press seams open and press in half lengthwise.

5 Sew the raw edges of the binding to the pinned tablecloth on the wrong side, referring to the general instructions for applying binding in the Basic Quilting Lessons. Turn the binding to the right side of the tablecloth and machine stitch in place using a small zigzag stitch.

If you choose not to bind the tablecloth, you can stitch the front and back, right sides together, leaving an opening to turn. Turn right side out and press. Fold in the open edge ¼" on both sides of the opening and edge stitch around all sides.

Napkins

Holiday

Everyday

*Whether using holiday or everyday colors,
these napkins can add a touch of spice to your holiday table setting.*

Napkins

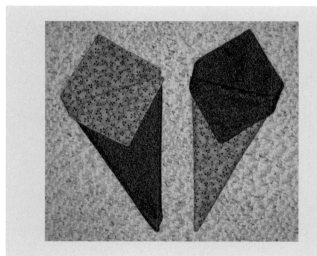

❄ Materials

(makes 4 reversible napkins)

1 yd. each two coordinating prints
Coordinating thread

❄ Cutting Instructions

(4) 17½" squares from first print
(4) 17½" squares from second print

❄ Directions

1 Cut two 17½" squares for each napkin. These squares can be cut from the same fabric, or two coordinating fabrics.

2 Place the squares, right sides together and pin around all the edges.

3 Sew around all four sides, using a ¼" seam allowance and leaving a 3"-4" opening to turn.

4 Turn the napkin right side out. Press the opening in ¼" on both the front and back pieces and pin.

5 Using an edge-stitch foot, if possible, stitch close to the edge around all four sides of the napkin. This will close the opening and give the edges some stability.

Everyone has different styles of decorating for the holidays. You can choose a monochromatic look or the traditional red and green combinations.

A blue napkin ring made from a motif print holds a blue napkin.

Our kitty color consultant prefers the red colorway, but you might want to mix and match them.

Place Mat, Table Runner & Hot Pads

Holiday

Every Day

Deck the halls and your tabletop too, with these festive red pieces to complement your green tablecloth. Set a striking holiday table with a runner and place mats. Set hot casseroles on the insulated pads, or use them to transport hot dishes to your holiday table.

SECTION 3A

Holiday Place Mat

Using the snowstripe print shown allows for fussy cutting the triangle and trapezoid pieces for a set of four place mats. As a bonus, there is enough fabric leftover to cut the smaller triangles for a set of four hot pads or pot holders.

Finished Size: 13" x 17½"
Skill Level: Beginner

❄ Materials (makes 4 place mats)

2¾ yd. red snowflake print
    (for backing and binding)
2 yd. red snowstripe print
Four 15" x 20" pieces batting

Template plastic
Permanent marker
Coordinating threads for piecing and quilting

❄ Cutting Instructions

Patterns for the triangles and trapezoid shapes are on the pattern sheet. Trace the template shapes with permanent marker on the template plastic. Refer to the cutting diagrams below to cut the following shapes using these templates.

Cutting diagram for triangles and trapezoids. Also shown are the smaller triangles for hot pads.

Red snowflake print
- (4) 15" x 20" pieces for backing
- (8) 2" x WOF strips for binding

Red snowstripe print
- 24 identical triangles
- 8 identical trapezoids

If you decide to use a different border print, you may have to adjust the yardage depending on the repeat of the stripe.

❄ Sewing Instructions

1 Referring to the place mat layout diagram, sew together three triangles to form one end. Repeat.

2 Sew the two trapezoid pieces, right sides together on the short end as shown.

3 Sew the two end pieces to the center, using the inset seam method. Repeat to make four place mats.

4 Layer the backing, batting and place mat top and quilt as desired. The place mat pictured was quilted around the outside and inside stripe details.

5 Sew the 2" binding strips together into pairs and bind each place mat, using your favorite method and referring to the Basic Quilting Lessons for hints on mitering the corners.

Placement diagram for triangles and trapezoids

Piecing diagram showing triangles sewn together on each side and trapezoid pieces sewn together

Using just the basic triangle pattern, you can create place mats in any fabric to complement your dining room or kitchen décor. These place mats are a little easier to sew as they are constructed of only triangles with no inset seams.

SECTION 3B

Everyday Place Mat

Finished Size: 13" x 17½"
Skill Level: Beginner

If you are not cutting the binding on the bias, you can cut two 2" x WOF strips of your binding fabric for each place mat. The sample shown has bias binding added as a design element.

❄ Materials (makes 4 place mats)

Fat quarter salmon dot print
Fat quarter brown stripe (for binding)
¾ yd. brown floral print
1 yd. salmon print (for backing)

❄ Cutting Instructions

Patterns for the triangles are on the pattern sheet. Trace the template shape with permanent marker on the template plastic. Refer to the cutting instructions below to cut the following shapes using this template.

Salmon print
(4) 15" x 20" pieces for backing
(8) 2" x WOF strips for binding

Salmon dot print
24 triangles

Brown floral print
24 identical triangles

Brown stripe
Cut 2" bias strips at a 45-degree angle across the fat quarter

❄ Sewing Instructions

1 Referring to the place mat layout diagram, sew together four triangles to form one end. Repeat.

Place mat layout diagram

2 Sew a salmon triangle to a brown triangle as shown. Repeat.

3 Join the two center sets together.

4 Sew the two end pieces to the center. Repeat to make four place mats.

5 Layer the backing, batting and place mat top and quilt as desired. The place mat pictured was quilted in the ditch between the triangles and again echoing the triangles several times. The center was quilted echoing the diamond shape.

6 Sew the 2" bias binding strips together to measure 60" for each place mat. Use your favorite method for sewing on the binding and referring to the Basic Quilting Lessons for hints on mitering the corners.

Using the same pattern pieces as for the place mat and elongating the center trapezoid pieces allows you to create a custom table runner to coordinate with the holiday place mats made in Section 3B.

SECTION 3C

Holiday Table Runner

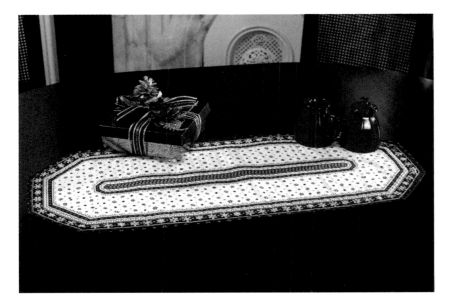

Finished Size: 13" x 34"
Skill Level: Beginner

❄ Materials (makes one)

1½ yd. red snowstripe print
1½ yd. red snowflake print
15" x 36" piece batting

Template plastic or paper
Permanent marker
Coordinating threads for piecing and quilting

❄ Cutting Instructions

Patterns for the triangles and trapezoid shapes are on the pattern sheet. Refer to the illustration. Trace the template shapes with permanent marker on the template plastic. Refer to the cutting diagrams below to cut the following shapes using these templates.

Red snowstripe print

(see cutting diagram)

    6 identical triangles
    2 trapezoid pieces to match the
        triangles

Red snowflake print

    (1) 15" x 36" piece for backing
    (3) 2" x WOF strips for binding

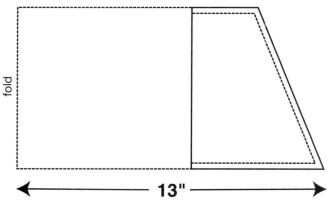

Trapezoid template using the elongated 13" for the table runner.

The table runner is pieced together exactly the same as the place mats. The only difference is in the size of the trapezoid pieces. Refer to the place mat section for illustrations.

❄ Sewing Instructions

1 Referring to the place mat layout diagram, sew together three triangles to form one end. Repeat.

2 Sew the two trapezoid pieces, right sides together on the short end as shown.

3 Sew the two end pieces to the center, using the inset seam method described on page 82.

4 Layer the backing, batting and table runner top and quilt as desired. The table runner pictured was quilted around the outside and inside stripe details.

5 Sew three 2" binding strips together into one binding strip and bind the table runner, using your favorite method and referring to the Basic Instruction Section for hints on mitering the corners.

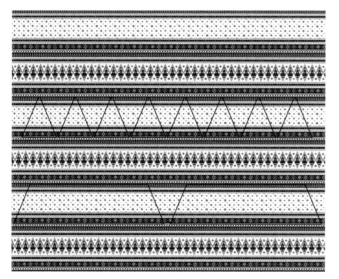

Cutting diagram for cutting identical triangles and trapezoids.

Everyday Table Runner

Finished Size: 13" x 34"
Skill Level: Beginner

❄ Materials (makes one)

Fat quarter salmon floral print
1⅛ yd. salmon dot print (includes backing)
½ yd. brown stripe (for bias binding)
1 yd. brown floral print
15" x 36" piece batting

Template plastic or paper
Permanent marker
Paper-backed fusible web
Coordinating threads for piecing and quilting

❄ Cutting Instructions

Refer to the holiday version for details on elongating the trapezoid template for the table runner.

Salmon dot print
(1) 15" x 35" piece for backing
4 triangles

Brown floral print
2 trapezoid pieces
2 triangles

Salmon floral print
1 appliqué piece (see sidebar)

Brown stripe
Cut 2" strips at a 45-degree angle across the yardage for bias binding

One quarter of the center appliqué design.

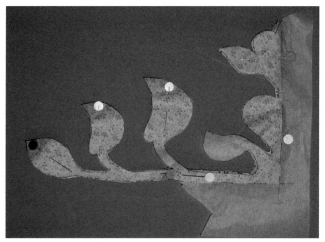

The appliqué before opening. You can see some of the pattern paper is still attached on the folded sides.

If you are not using bias binding, sew three 2" x WOF strips together to bind the table runner.

❋ Sewing Instructions

The table runner is pieced together exactly the same as the holiday version. The only difference is the addition of the fused appliqué motif.

1 Follow steps 1 - 3 for the Holiday Table Runner.

2 Following manufacturer's instructions, fuse the web to the wrong side of the salmon floral fat quarter. Using the pattern provided for the quarter appliqué design, trace a paper pattern. Fold the fabric in half horizontally and then in half vertically. Pin the paper pattern to this folded piece and carefully cut on the traced lines.

3 Center the appliqué motif on the brown center of the table runner and fuse in place, following manufacturer's instructions.

4 Layer your backing, batting and table runner and quilt as desired. The sample pictured was quilted with echoing triangles on the ends and around the motif in the center. Use a zigzag or buttonhole stitch around all outside edges while quilting the motif.

5 Sew the 2" bias binding strips together to measure approximately 95" for the table runner. Use your favorite method for sewing on the binding and referring to the Basic Instruction Section for hints on mitering the corners.

*Everyone can use several hot pads or potholders for holiday entertaining.
By fussy cutting this snowstripe print we have optimized its use in
making four sets of place mats and hot pads.*

Holiday Hot Pad

Use the pattern provided for the triangle, cutting the smaller version for the hot pad. In the sample shown we used some of the leftover yardage from the snowstripe print to cut the triangles and binding.

❄ Materials (makes four)

Piece of red snowstripe print leftover from
   the place mat yardage
¾ yd. of red print (for backing)
⅝ yd. binding fabric

Template plastic or paper
(4) 12" squares heat resistant batting or a
   double layer of heavy cotton batting

❄ Cutting Instructions

Red snowstripe print
32 identical triangles from the smaller triangle template

Binding fabric
(10) 2" x WOF strips

❄ Sewing Instructions

1 Sew the triangles together in pairs as shown.

2 Sew two pairs together to make one half of the hot pad. Repeat.

3 Sew the two halves together.

4 Layer the backing, batting and hot pad and quilt as desired. The sample pictured was quilted around the center star motif and around some of the geometric lines on the outside.

5 Piece the binding strips and bind as desired. Repeat to make a total of four hot pads.

These hot pads make great hostess gifts.

Refer to the Holiday Place Mat section to see the fabric layout diagram where these triangles were cut on the snowstripe print.

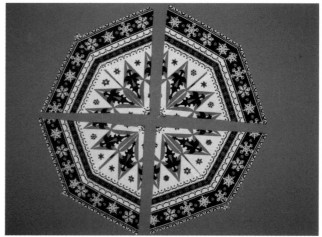

Make four pairs.

Press seams in one direction, except when assembling the two halves. To reduce bulk, we suggest pressing the last seam open.

*It's always nice to have matching hot pads for everyday use.
Make several with leftover fabric from your projects
and give away as gifts during the year.*

Everyday Hot Pad

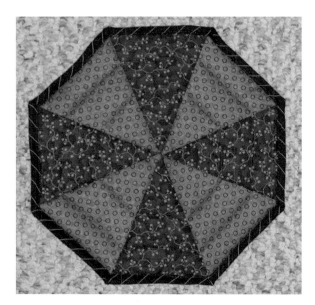

*Once again, we used leftover fabric
from the place mat and table runner.*

❋ Materials (makes four)

Piece of salmon dot print
Piece of brown floral print
Three 2" x WOF strips for binding
(or use some leftover bias strips
from previous projects)

Template plastic or paper
(4) 12" squares heat resistant batting or a
double layer of heavy cotton batting

❄ Cutting Instructions

Salmon dot print
4 triangles from the smaller triangle template

Brown floral print
4 triangles from the smaller triangle template

Binding fabric
(3) 2" x WOF strips

❄ Sewing Instructions

1 Sew the triangles together in pairs as shown.

2 Sew two pairs together to make one half of the hot pad. Repeat.

3 Sew the two halves together.

4 Layer the backing, batting and hot pad and quilt as desired. The sample pictured was quilted around the center in a repeating octagonal grid.

5 Piece the binding strips and bind as desired.

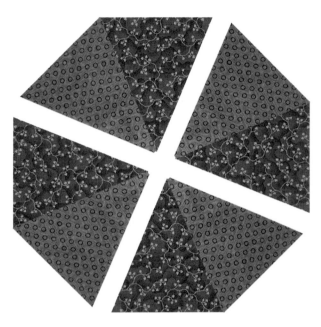

Make four pairs.

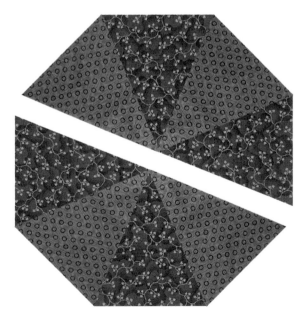

Press seams in one direction, except when assembling the two halves. To reduce bulk, we suggest pressing the last seam open.

The Bedroom

Brighten your holiday season and decorate your bedroom for the winter
with this queen size bed quilt in shades of green. Adding a fabric shade and pillowcases
completes the coordinated look. Subdued elegance describes the everyday version of this
bedroom ensemble in elegant shades of salmon and chocolate. Complete the room décor
with wall sconces and dimensional desk accessories.

Bed Quilts

Holiday

Everyday

Quilting

The winter print shown is not holiday specific, so this quilt can be used throughout the entire winter season. The leprechauns in your house might enjoy this quilt until St. Patrick's Day. The alternate colorway for the everyday version features a plain alternate block, which gives you a space to highlight some special quilting designs.

SECTION 1A

Winter Holiday Bed Quilt

Crisscross heart designs surround a winter tree motif in the alternate blocks. Use this charming border print featuring silhouettes of children frolicking in the snow to complete the winter look.

Finished Quilt Size: 95" x 95" (queen)
Finished Block Size: 10"
Skill Level: Advanced Beginner/
Intermediate

Other border prints are readily available to use in this type of design. If you wish to use a different border, calculate the width of the selected border design and adjust the inner and outer border strips to fit your bed.

Materials

¼ yd. reindeer print

3 yd. diamond tree print (inner border, sashing, block background)

3 yd. tree motif print (fussy cut blocks)

3 yd. silhouette stripe (mitered outer borders - see sidebar)

3½ yd. snowflake print (heart Block A, nine patches, sashing cornerstones, middle and outer borders, binding)

100" x 100" backing fabric

100" x 100" piece of cotton/poly batting

Rotary cutter, mat and ruler

Threads in colors to match fabrics for piecing and quilting

Basic sewing supplies

Cutting Instructions

Reindeer print

(3) 2½" strips; subcut into (16) 2½" x 6½" pieces

Snowflake print

(13) 3" strips; subcut into (32) 3" squares (reserve 10 for outer border)

(24) 2½" x WOF strips; subcut 2 strips into (25) 2½" cornerstone squares and subcut 6 strips into (32) 2½" x 6½" rectangles for Block A (reserve 8 strips for nine-patches and 8 strips for middle border)

(10) 2" x WOF strips for binding

Diamond tree print

(4) 10½" x WOF strips; subcut into 60 10½" x 2½" sashing strips

(2) 4½" strips; subcut into 16 4½" squares

(3) 3" strips; subcut into 32 3" squares

(15) 2½" x WOF; reserve 7 for nine-patches and 8 for inner borders

Tree motif print

(16) 10½" squares

Silhouette stripe

(4) 6¾" x 92" lengthwise border strips for outside border (See sidebar on page 97 if not mitering corners)

ꝺ Sewing Instructions

If you prefer to sew straight borders instead of mitering, they can be cut at 78½". Or, measure your quilt top across the center in both directions to get an average. Since everyone's seam allowance can be a little different, there may be a difference in overall size of the quilt. If you decide to sew straight borders, you can reduce your fabric yardage to 2⅓ yd.

Heart Block A

1 Sew a snowflake print 2½" strip to either side of a diamond tree print 2½" strip. Press seams toward the snowflake print. Repeat to make a total of three strip sets. Subcut into 40 Unit A 2½" pieces. See diagram 1.

2 Sew a diamond tree print 2½" strip to either side of a snowflake print 2½" strip. Press seams toward the snowflake. Repeat to make a total of two strip sets. Subcut into 20 Unit B 2½" pieces. See diagram 2.

3 Referring to diagram 3, sew two of the Unit A pieces to one of the Unit B pieces, matching seams. Make a total of 20 nine-patch blocks (reserve four for Block B).

4 Mark a diagonal line on the back of the diamond tree 3" squares.

5 Place a diamond tree print square on top of a snowflake print 3" square, right sides together. Sew ¼" from the drawn line on both sides. Cut apart on the line and press toward the darker fabric. Repeat to make a total of 64 half square triangle units. Trim to measure 2½" square. See Diagram 4.

Diagram 1

Diagram 2

Diagram 3

Diagram 4

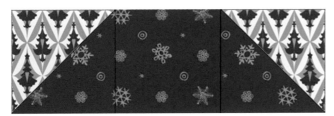

Diagram 5

6 Referring to Diagram 5, sew two of these half-square triangles to either side of a 2½" snowflake square. Repeat to make a total of 32 Unit C pieces.

Diagram 6

7 Sew each of these units to a 2½" x 6½" snowflake rectangle. See Diagram 6.

Block A Diagram

8 Referring to the Block A Diagram, assemble the block, using one 4½" diamond tree square, one nine-patch and two of the Unit C pieces. Make a total of 16 blocks.

Make a nine-block quilt for a coordinating wall hanging with four Block A, one Block B and four 10½" square Tree blocks. One block with a border makes a charming throw pillow.

Block B

1 Sew a snowflake 2½" square to either end of a deer print 2½" x 6½" rectangle. Repeat to make eight pieces. See Diagram 7.

Diagram 7

2 Use four nine-patch units reserved from Block A above to assemble the block. Refer to the Block B Diagram to assemble using one nine-patch, two deer rectangles and two of the units made in step #1 above. Make four blocks.

Block B Diagram

Quilt Assembly

1 Following the Quilt Layout Diagram, sew the blocks together in rows, with diamond tree print 10½" x 2½" vertical sashing pieces between all the blocks.

2 Sew a row of six diamond tree sashing strips with five snowflake 2½" corner squares. Repeat to make a total of five pieced sashing rows.

3 Referring to the Quilt Layout Diagram, sew the rows together, with pieced sashing strips between all rows.

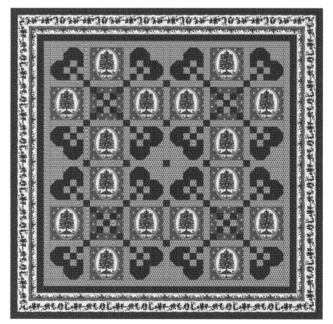

Quilt Layout Diagram

Adding Borders

1 Sew the remaining eight diamond tree 2½" strips together in pairs for the sashing borders. Stitch to the sides of the quilt. Press and trim excess. Sew the final two strips to the top and bottom.

2 Sew the snowflake 2½" border strips together in pairs and attach to the quilt in the same manner as the step above.

3 Fold the 92" silhouette border strips in half lengthwise and mark. Also mark the center of the quilt top.

4 Pin the strips in place, matching up the marked center of the silhouette border strip with the center of the quilt on each side and pinning to the outside. That will give you approximately 7" extra length on either side to miter the corners.

5 Sew the strips in place, starting and stopping ¼" from the end of each side. Press the seams toward the quilt top.

6 Refer to the Quilting Lesson section for mitering the border strips.

7 Join two of the green snowflake 3" border strips, short ends together. Repeat to make four strips.

8 Cut two of the green snowflake 3" border strips in half and stitch the half strips to the strips pieced in step 7.

9 Attach these strips to the outside of the quilt top.

Close-up of the mitered corner.

Finishing

1 Layer the backing, batting and quilt top and quilt as desired. The quilt pictured was quilted with diagonal lines across the nine-patches, around the oval tree motifs and with allover swirls in the borders. The silhouette border was quilted along the geometric lines.

2 Square up the quit top, trimming the outside border to measure 2".

3 Bind with the 2" green snowflake fabric, using your favorite method. Refer to the binding instructions in the Quilting Lessons.

Refer to the What Color is Your Holiday? section on page 123 for alternate color possibilities for this holiday quilt

Fashionable shades of salmon and chocolate will find favor with women.
These same colors will suggest coziness, comfort and warmth to the man of the house.
A home décor that everyone can agree on. The window coverings and desk accessories
would create a comfortable look in a home office, as well.

SECTION 1B

Love is All Around Bed Quilt

Finished Quilt Size: 94" x 94" (queen)
Finished Block Size: 10"
Skill Level: Advanced Beginner/
Intermediate

You can choose colors to coordinate with any bedroom for this simple design.

Materials

1 yd. chocolate vines
1½ yd. brown stripe (sashing)
1½ yd. salmon twigs
1½ yd. salmon dots (inner border and
   binding)
2¼ yd. tan arrows
2¾ yd. chocolate spikes (middle border)

100" x 100" backing fabric
100" x 100" piece of batting
Rotary cutter, mat and ruler
Threads in colors to match fabrics for piecing
Thread for piecing and quilting
Basic sewing supplies

Cutting Instructions

Salmon twigs print

(15) 2½" x WOF strips; subcut 6 into
(32) 2½" x 6½" pieces and 2
into (32) 2½" squares (reserve the
remaining strips for nine-patches)
(3) 3" x WOF strips; subcut into 32
3" squares

Chocolate vines print

(10) 2½" x WOF strips; subcut 2 strips into
(25) 2½" squares (reserve the
remaining strips for nine-patches)

Tan arrows print

(16) 10½" squares
(2) 4½" strips; subcut into (16) 4½" squares
(3) 3" strips; subcut into (32) 3" squares

*The middle border strips were cut lengthwise
from this fabric to avoid fussy cutting and
piecing the motif. If you prefer to cut your strips
across the width of the fabric, you can reduce the
yardage to 2¼ yd. Cut ten 7½" x WOF strips
and piece them to the measurements in the
cutting instructions.*

Brown stripe

(15) 2½" x WOF strips; subcut into (60)
2½" x 10½" pieces for sashing

Salmon dots print

(8) 3½" x WOF strips for inner border
(10) 2" x WOF strips for binding

Chocolate spikes print

(2) 7½" x 80½" lengthwise strips for side
middle border
(2) 7½" x 96½" lengthwise strips for top
and bottom middle border

❧ Sewing Instructions

Block A

1 Sew a chocolate vine 2½" strip to either side of a salmon twigs 2½" strip. Press seams toward the chocolate. Repeat to make a total of three strip sets. Subcut into 32 Unit A 2½" pieces. See Diagram 1.

2 Sew a salmon twigs 2½" strip to either side of a chocolate vine 2½" strip. Press seams toward the chocolate. Repeat to make a total of two strip sets. Subcut into 32 Unit B 2½" pieces. See Diagram 2.

3 Referring to Diagram 3, sew two of the Unit A pieces to one of the Unit B pieces, matching seams. Make a total of 20 nine-patch blocks (reserve four for Block B).

4 Mark a diagonal line on the back of the salmon 3" squares.

5 Place a salmon square on top of a tan arrow 3" square, right sides together. Sew ¼" from the drawn line on both sides. Cut apart on the line and press toward the darker fabric. Repeat to make a total of 64 half-square triangle units. Trim to measure 2½" square. See Diagram 4.

6 Referring to Diagram 5, sew two of these half-square triangles to either side of a 2½" salmon square. Repeat to make a total of 32 Unit C pieces.

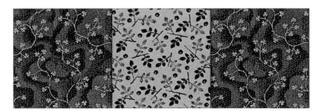

Diagram 1

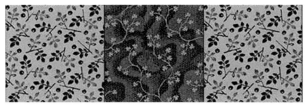

Diagram 2

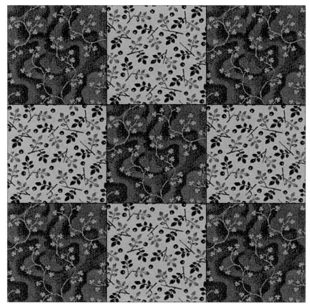

Diagram 3

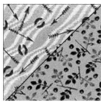 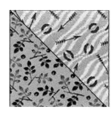

Diagram 4

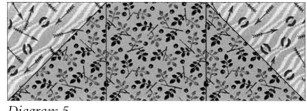

Diagram 5

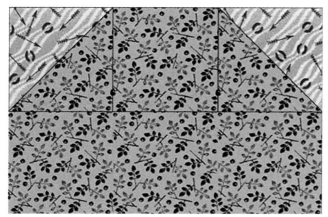

Diagram 6

7 Sew each of these units to a 2½" x 6½" salmon rectangle.

8 Referring to the Block A Diagram, assemble the block using one 4½" tan square, one nine-patch and two of the Unit C pieces. Make a total of 16 blocks.

Block B

1 Sew a chocolate vines 2½" square to either end of a tan arrows 2½" x 6½" rectangle. Repeat to make eight pieces. See Diagram 7.

2 Use four nine-patch units reserved from Block A above to assemble the block. Refer to the Block B Diagram to assemble, using one nine-patch, two tan rectangles and two of the units made in step #1 above. Make four blocks.

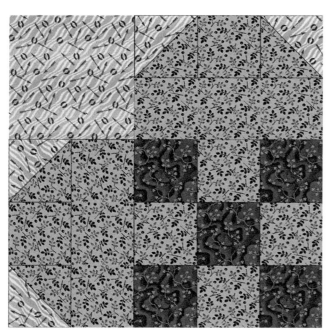

Block A Diagram

Diagram 7

Block B Diagram

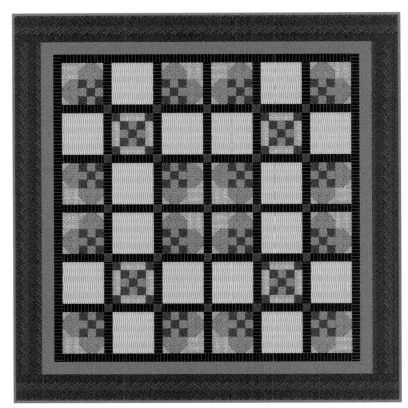

Quilt Layout Diagram

Quilt Assembly

1 Following the Quilt Layout Diagram, sew the blocks together in rows, with chocolate stripe 10½" x 2½" vertical sashing pieces between all the blocks.

2 Sew a row of six chocolate stripe sashing strips with five chocolate vines 2½" corner squares. Repeat to make a total of five pieced sashing rows.

3 Sew the rows together, with these pieced sashing strips between all rows, referring to the Quilt Layout Diagram.

Adding Borders

1 Sew the remaining 2½" chocolate stripe pieces together in pairs for the sashing borders. Stitch to the sides of the quilt. Press and trim excess. Sew the final two strips to the top and bottom.

2 Sew the salmon dots 3½" border strips together in pairs and attach to the quilt in the same manner as the step above.

3 Sew the chocolate spikes 7½" border strips together in pairs. Cut one chocolate spikes border strip in half and sew to the end of two of these pieced border strips. Attach the shorter strips to the sides. Press and trim excess. Attach the longer strips to the top and bottom. Press and trim.

Finishing

1 Layer the backing, batting and quilt top and quilt as desired. The quilt pictured was quilted with a floral motif in the blocks, a leaf pattern in the sashing and hearts and flowers in the borders.

2 Square the quilt and bind with the 2" stripe fabric, using your favorite method. Refer to binding in the Basic Quilting Lessons.

SECTION 2

Pillowcases

Holiday

Everyday

Custom pillowcases are so simple to make, you'll wonder why you haven't made them to match all your bed quilts. They can be made with contrasting borders and folded inset pieces as shown here. You can also eliminate the folded strip and just use two different fabrics for the main and border pieces. Your third choice is to cut the border piece from the same main fabric and insert a folded trim strip of a coordinating color. Imagine the possibilities!

SECTION 2

Standard Pillowcase

Complete the coordinated bed ensemble with matching pillowcases. Instructions are provided for standard, queen and king size to accommodate any size bed pillows. The pillows in the photographs are standard, queen and king size.

Finished Size: 35"

Materials

Main Fabric: 26" x WOF
Trim Fabric: 2" x WOF (fold in half lengthwise)
Border Fabric: 10½" x WOF

ꙮ Sewing Instructions

1 Place the raw edges of the folded trim fabric along the right side of one of the long edges of the main fabric. Lay the border fabric on top of the trim, right sides together. Pin all layers and sew ¼" seam through all four layers. Press the seam toward the border.

2 Trim the side edges of all fabrics along the side seam to even it up. With right sides together, seam the side and bottom edges, matching the seams of the border pieces.

3 Turn under ¼" along the raw edge of the border and press. Fold the pressed edge of the border inside, press and pin to the border to cover the seam line. Topstitch from the right side to secure the border. You can stitch on either the border or the trim. Try using a decorative machine stitch and contrasting thread for an additional design element.

For larger sizes, cut the fabrics to the sizes listed and follow the directions above.

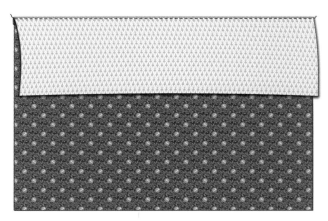

Three components to pillowcase — main fabric, folded contrasting trim strip and coordinating border piece.

Queen Size Pillowcase
Finished Size: 40"

Materials
Main Fabric: 30" x WOF
Trim Fabric: 2" x WOF strip
   (fold in half lengthwise)
Border Fabric: 10½" x WOF

King Size Pillowcase
Finished Size: 44"

Materials
Main Fabric: 34" x WOF
Trim Fabric: 2" x WOF strip
   (fold in half lengthwise)
Border Fabric: 10½" x WOF

Layers showing pillowcase main fabric, top with folded trim strip and border fabric.

Home Office Accessories

Holiday

Everyday

Avoid clutter on your desk or night stand by creating coordinated containers. Design your own desk accessories, making several different sizes and shapes in fabrics to coordinate with your bedroom, office or foyer. These pieces are offered in several sizes and shapes to store and organize your bills and letters, remotes, electronic devices and even keys and loose change.

SECTION 3A

Letter Caddy

Follow the basic fusing, cutting and assembly instructions in the Family Room Chapter beginning on page 41 for making these dimensional accessories. Below are the fabric requirements for the final versions.

Finished Container Size:
Approximately 9½" x 3" x 3¾"
Skill Level: Beginner/Intermediate

Materials

Everyday Version

Fat quarter brown floral print
Fat quarter salmon arrow print
12" x 19" piece Timtex
(2) 12" x 19" pieces fusible interfacing
Coordinating threads

Holiday Version

Fat quarter green deer print
Fat quarter green snowflake print
12" x 19" piece Timtex
(2) 12" x 19" pieces fusible interfacing
Coordinating threads

Window Treatments

Holiday

Everyday

Have you admired that custom look you see in home décor magazines?
Here's a way to create designer looks with coordinated roll-up fabric shades and valances.
There are many ways to style these, using either coordinating or contrasting fabrics for
very different looks. Use the shades alone for one look or top with a valance for another.
Use the layered valance to top a window with shutters or café curtains. Once again, we
have tried to spark your imagination to create unique looks for your home.

SECTION 4A

Holiday Roll-Up Fabric Shade

You can use the shade as it is, or top it with a valance. Imagine a new look for every season and every room of your home. Our green holiday version will be in season through St. Patrick's day.

Size: 36" x 48"
Skill Level: Beginner

Materials (will make one window shade)

1⅛ yd. border stripe print
1½ yd. green tree diamond print
1½ yd. green deer print
1" x 34" wooden dowel (½" diameter) for the bottom pocket
Hanging rod and brackets of your choice for hanging the shade
Coordinating threads

ꙮ Cutting Instructions

From the border print

(1) 8½" x 37" lengthwise strip

(2) 4" x 36" lengthwise strips*

(2) 4" x 40" lengthwise strips*

* The strips for the back ties are cut a little longer than the front because when the shade is rolled, the back ties have to come around the roll to meet the ties in the front.

From the green tree diamond print

(1) 36½" x 48½" rectangle

From the green deer print

(1) 36½" x 48½" rectangle

To use a different border print, purchase enough fabric for a strip between 9" and 10" in width and 36" in length. This piece is for the rod pocket on top of the shade. You will also need two 4" x 36" and two 4" x 40" strips for the ties. A 1⅛ yd. piece is generally sufficient to cut these five pieces. Adjust the cutting of the width of the border strips according to the pattern on your fabric. The top rod pocket and the ties can be flexible in their finished size, according to the scale of your border print.

ꙮ Sewing Instructions

1 Sew the green tree diamond and green deer pieces, right sides together at the 48" sides and around the bottom, referring to Diagram 1. If you have a directional print, be sure to face it up on the front and down on the back. When the shade is rolled up, the back will then appear right side up. Clip corners and turn right side out. Press.

Diagram 1

2 Fold the back up 1½" at the bottom edge of the shade (seamed edge) to create a rod pocket. Pin and stitch across the width, close to the seam. See Diagram 2.

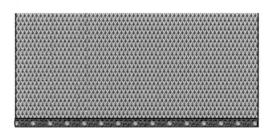

Diagram 2

3 Sew hems on the sides of the 8½" x 37" border print rectangle by folding in ¼" and then again ¼". Stitch to secure as shown in Diagram 3. This rod pocket should measure 4" x 36".

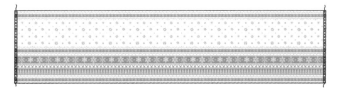

Diagram 3

4 Fold the border print 4" tie strips, right sides together and stitch the long sides on all four strips. Turn to right side and press with the seam in the back.

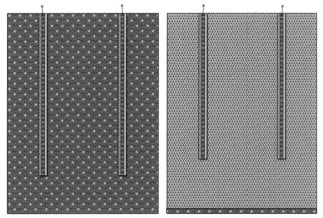

5 Finish the bottom edges of these ties by turning the raw edges inside ½" and top stitching.

Diagram 4
Ties should line up in the front and back, approximately 7½" from each side.

6 Referring to Diagram 4, line up the raw edges of the two longer ties 7½" in from each side and pin. Pin the two shorter ties for the front, lining up with the ties pinned to the back and baste everything in place.

7 With raw edges and right sides together, sew one side of the rod pocket strip to the back of the shade, keeping the ties flat and straight. See Diagram 5

Diagram 5
Stitch all the pieces together from the back of the shade.

8 Press ¼" in on the remaining raw edge of the rod pocket, fold over to the right side of the shade and top stitch in place, covering the previous stitching line. See Diagram 6.

Diagram 6

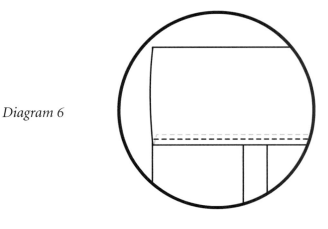

9 Insert the wooden dowel into the bottom of the shade. This will create a shade bottom that is supported to roll up to the desired length on the window.

10 Insert the hanging rod into the top pocket and hang the shade on your window.

11 After you have hung the shade on your window, determine the length you want the shade to be, roll it up and secure with the ties on either side. Tie in an attractive bow or knot, stand back and admire your handiwork.

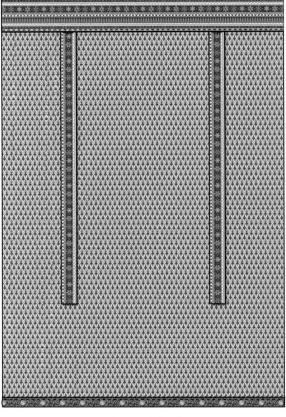

Front of shade

Imagine creating these coordinated shades for seasonal change in your rooms.
Attractive in any color combinations, you can easily rotate from room to room,
or change to match any color whim.

Everyday Roll-Up Fabric Shade

Size: 36" x 48"
Skill Level: Beginner

Materials (will make one window shade)

1 ¼ yd. brown stripe print

1 ⅜ yd. salmon dot print

1 ⅜ yd. tan stripe print

1" x 33" wooden dowel (⅓" diameter) for the
   bottom pocket

Hanging rod and brackets of your choice for
   hanging the shade

Coordinating threads

Cutting Instructions

From the brown stripe print

(1) 8½" x 37" lengthwise strip
(2) 4" x 36" lengthwise strips *
(2) 4" x 40" lengthwise strips *

From the salmon dot print

(1) 36½" x 48½" rectangle

From the tan stripe print

(1) 36½" x 48½" rectangle

Sewing Instructions

1 Follow the instructions above for the Holiday Fabric Shade, substituting the everyday fabrics.

2 Use the 8½" x 37" salmon dot and tan stripe pieces in place of the green diamond and green deer pieces to construct the basic shade.

3 Sew hems on the sides of the brown stripe print 8½" x 37" rectangle, following the instructions for the border print rectangle.

4 Fold and stitch the brown stripe 4" tie strips, following the instructions for the border print ties.

5 Line up ties and finish construction of the shade, following Steps 6 through 11 for the Holiday Fabric Shade.

Use the same basic pattern piece from the Mantel Cover in the Family Room Section to create unique window toppers which will harmonize with your fabric shades.

SECTION 4C

Holiday Window Valance
Finished Size: 40" wide
Length from 10" to 14½"

Each one of these flaps measures 10" finished, so you can add or subtract units or overlap them to create a custom fit for your window. The rod pocket is easily lengthened or shortened to accommodate different size windows.

Materials (makes one valance)

½ yd. green snowflake print *

¼ yd. green tree diamond print *

1¾ yd. green deer print *

3 yd. tracing paper 12" wide

Permanent marker

Hanging rod and brackets of your choice for hanging the valance

Coordinating threads

* see sidebar for fabric requirement explanation

Cutting Instructions

Tree diamond print

(3) 2½" x WOF strips

Green snowflake print

(3) 2½" x WOF strips
(1) 8½" x 41" strip (for rod pocket)

Deer print

2 piece A   4 piece B
2 piece C   4 piece D

Sewing Instructions

1 Using the patterns on the pattern sheet, trace the following pieces onto the tracing paper, using a permanent marker. Roughly cut out the patterns. You will need a total of two each of traced paper patterns A, B, C and D, making sure to trace the stitching line as well as the cutting line.

If you use a pencil or ballpoint pen when tracing your pattern pieces, it's possible that the pencil or pen marks could transfer to your fabric below when stitching in Step 3. We recommend using only permanent markers and allowing them to dry before stitching.

Diagram 1

2 Make a strip set consisting of three green snowflake 2½" pieces and two green tree diamond 2½" pieces as shown in the diagram. Strip set should measure 10½" x WOF as per Diagram 1.

3 Place the strip set fabric right sides together with the deer print backing fabric and pin the paper templates for piece A and C in place. Refer to Diagram 2. Carefully cut apart between the units.

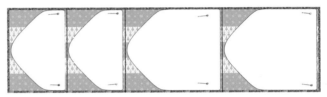

Diagram 2
Deer print backing fabric is right side up, strip set is wrong side up and patterns pinned in place on top.

*This fabric requirement assumes that you will get at least four pattern repeats across the yardage after piecing the strip sets. Also measure your background fabric to make sure you can cut four patterns across the width. To be safe, you can purchase ¼ yd. of each of the first two fabrics and 1⅓ yd. of the background. That will allow for making an extra strip set, if necessary and cutting an additional pattern piece if you can only fit 3 across your yardage. Since fabrics vary so greatly in finished size (also depending on whether or not you pre-wash), we have tried to estimate sufficient yardage to complete these projects successfully.

4 Take each unit to the sewing machine and stitch down the sides and around the bottom on the inside line, which is your ¼" seam line. Secure the beginning and end of your seam line to reinforce for turning the piece right side out. Leave the top open for turning. Clip curves. See Diagram 3.

5 Tear the paper away, turn to the right side and press.

6 Repeat this process to make the B and D units pinning the paper patterns on two layers of 12" strips of deer print fabric, right sides together.

7 Referring to Diagram 4, sew hems on the short sides of the green snowflake print 8½" x 41" rectangle by folding in ¼" and then again ¼". Stitch to secure. Fold in half lengthwise with wrong sides together and press as shown. Baste with a long machine stitch on the raw edge. This rod pocket should measure 4¼" x 40".

8 Layer the flaps as shown, with the A and C strip-pieced flaps on top of the deer print background B and C flaps and baste them together with a continuous stitch so the pieces are all held together in order. Each flap should measure 10" finished and fit exactly across the width of the rod pocket.

9 With right sides together, sew one side of the rod pocket strip to the back of the flaps.

10 Press ¼" on the remaining raw edge of the rod pocket, fold over to the right sides of the valance and pin the rod pocket in place.

11 Top stitch from the front side, covering the previous stitching line and securing the rod pocket. Press and install on your window with the hanging rod.

Using the paper patterns helps to stabilize these pieces when you are stitching around curves. This is a helpful method to keep in mind when sewing other bias-edge pieces.

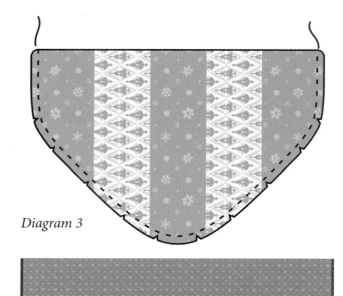

Diagram 3

Diagram 4
Hemming the rod pocket.

Diagram 5
Showing the flaps basted together in the proper order.

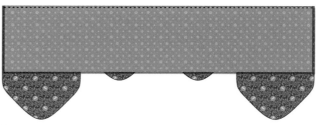

Diagram 6
Attaching the rod pocket to the back of the basted flaps.

Diagram 7
Folded edge top-stitched on the front of the valance.

*Once you try this simple pattern
you will want to make these valances to coordinate all your rooms.*

SECTION 4D

Everyday Window Valance
Finished Size: 40" wide
Length from 10" to 14½"

Ⓠ Materials (makes one valance)

½ yd. brown circle print

¾ yd. tan arrow print

½ yd. brown stripe pint

3 yd. Golden Threads or other tracing
 paper 12" wide

Permanent marker

Hanging rod and brackets of your choice
 for hanging the shade

Coordinating threads

⊘ Cutting Instructions

Read all instructions on pages 118-120 for the holiday version before beginning to cut and sew.

Brown stripe print

(1) 8½" x 41" strip (for rod pocket)

Brown circle print

(per instructions in Steps 3 - 6)
2 piece A
2 piece C

Tan arrow print

(per holiday version instructions in Steps 3 - 6)
2 piece A
2 piece C
4 piece B
4 piece D

If you want to hang the valance in conjunction with your fabric shade, purchase a double-tiered curtain rod and hang the shade on the inside rod and the valance on the outside rod.

⊘ Sewing Instructions

1 This window valance is constructed exactly the same as the holiday version, except using solid fabrics instead of strip sets for the top flaps.

2 Refer to those instructions, using the fabric references above to create window valances in these brown and tan fabrics.

3 In this case we have suggested using the brown circle print instead of the strip sets, the tan print in place of the deer print and the brown stripe in place of the green snowflake for the rod pocket.

What Color is Your Holiday?

Here is a two-color version of the Winter Holiday Bed Quilt for the red/green holiday traditionalist.

Another version for those who enjoy their holidays in crisp wintry blues.

As we thought about designing this line for holiday decorating, it occurred to us that although many folks enjoy decorating for Christmas with the traditional red and green, many more are interested in using fabrics that speak more of winter than a specific holiday. We included the blue colorway in this line as we have many Jewish friends who entertain and decorate during their holiday of Hanukkah, The Festival of Lights, which can occur in late November, December or even early January. We know of many households who wish to celebrate in both traditions in honor of the multicultural heritage of its family members. As a result, the line that we created features winter scenes of children playing, snowflakes, deer and trees typical of the winter season during which these holidays are celebrated.

Whether you are creating table décor, window treatments, desk-top accessories, throws or bedroom ensembles, we think you will find the Tannenbaum line of fabrics suitable for every taste, every mood and every tradition all winter long.

Tanya likes to choose her own favorite colorway. It seems that she prefers the red fabrics. We are planning to make her a new nap quilt for Christmas. What is the favorite color you prefer for your special holiday?

ℚ Resources

Our heartfelt thanks go to the suppliers who helped in the production of this book by providing products we used to create the samples shown in the previous pages.

Love In Stitches

P.O. Box 257
Pine Brook, NJ 07058
www.loveinstitches.com

Visit Barbara and Yolanda's website for a free wall hanging pattern that coordinates with the projects in this book.

Superior Threads

Bob & Heather Purcell
P.O. Box 1672
St. George, UT 84771
800-449-1777 or 435-652-1867

Heather Purcell is a master at choosing the correct color and type of thread for any project. We appreciate having her expertise in selecting and supplying the various types of thread we used in this book. They included Masterpiece, Bottom Line, MonoPoly clear invisible, So Fine, King Tut, Razzle Dazzle and Rainbow threads.

Colors suggested for Tannenbaum are:
  Bottom Line: 611 Turquoise, 612 Green and 627 Red
  So Fine: 413 Scarlet, 436 Midnight Harbor and
    443 Forest
  King Tut: 927 De Nile, 946 Rubiyah and 989 Malichite
  Metallic: 28 Jade, 35 Pacific Blue and 51 Cranberry
    or 62 Red
  Razzle Dazzle: 257 Ruby Slippers, 268 Blue Topaz
    and 275 Jazzy Jade

Windham Fabrics

Mickey Kreuger
812 Jersey Avenue
Jersey City, NJ 07310
201-659-0444
www.windhamfabrics.com

Windham supplied all the Tannenbaum fabrics used in this book, which they produced especially for this project. They also supplied the Salmon & Chocolate fabrics for the everyday projects featured throughout.

Mountain Mist

2551 Crescentville Road
Cincinnati, OH 45241
800-345-7150 or 513-326-3912
www.stearnstextiles.com

Our contact at Mountain Mist, Vickie Paullus, frequently makes suggestions about the types of batting which would be most useful in the different types of projects and different types of quilting being done on them. We appreciate all the support given to us by this company in supplying many different types of batting for us to use in the projects.

Batting used in the book included: Cotton Blossom in the Silk and Wool blends, White Rose, Gold Polyester Cotton Blend, Gold Fuse (50% Cotton/50% Poly) and White Gold (100% cotton) fusible batting. Visit their web site to see the full range of products offered for quilters.

Sullivan's USA

4341 Midcaugh Avenue
Downers Grove, IL 60515
800-862-8586
www.sullivans.net/usa/

We frequently use a quilt basting spray when layering the top, batting and backing for quilting on a domestic machine. Our favorite has been Sullivans Quilt Basting Spray, which comes in an economical 13 oz. can.

Tannenbaum fabrics used in these projects will be available for a limited time. Feel free to contact us with comments or questions.

Additional Resources

Annie's Attic
1 Annie Lane
Big Sandy, TX 75755
Phone: 800-582-6643
Web: www.anniesattic.com

Clotilde LLC
P.O. Box 7500
Big Sandy, TX 75755-7500
Phone: 800-772-2891
Web: www.clotilde.com

Connecting Threads
P.O. Box 870760
Vancouver, WA 98687-7760
Phone: 800-574-6454
Web: www.ConnectingThreads.com

Ghee's
2620 Centenary Blvd. No. 2-250
Shreveport, LA 71104
Phone: 318-226-1701
E-mail: bags@ghees.com
Web: www.ghees.com

Herrschners, Inc.
2800 Hoover Road
Stevens Point, WI 54492-0001
Phone: 800-441-0838
Web: www.herrschners.com

Home Sew
P.O. Box 4099
Bethlehem, PA 18018-0099
Phone: 800-344-4739
Web: www.homesew.com

Keepsake Quilting
Route 25
P.O. Box 1618
Center Harbor, NH 03226-1618
Phone: 800-438-5464
Web: www.keepsakequilting.com

Krause Publications
700 E. State St.
Iola, WI 54990
800-258-0929
Web: www.krausebooks.com

Nancy's Notions
333 Beichl Ave.
P.O. Box 683
Beaver Dam, WI 53916-0683
Phone: 800-833-0690
Web: www.nancysnotions.com

✑ Contributors

Without the help of these talented and creative ladies, it would have been impossible for us to accomplish so much in so little time. Thanks to all those listed here and for others who shall remain nameless for their valuable assistance.

Karen Anderson

Pieced the Holiday Bed Quilt

Raising two boys in Blairstown, working a full-time job and attending college part-time leaves Karen little spare time. Yet she was kind enough to volunteer to piece one of the largest projects for us with a very short deadline. Karen, Barbara and Yolanda are all members of the Garden State Quilt Guild, which meets in Morris County, NJ. Karen is not only a prolific quilter but was also in charge of the very successful yearly guild challenge projects for the past two years. The new one for 2007 looks like great fun, too.

Sue Mangina

Pieced and quilted the Everyday Lap Quilt

Living in Parsippany, N.J. with her husband Ross, Sue has been honing her quilting skills for several years. Her work is precise and her input on instructions much valued. Sue is also a member of the Garden State Quilt Guild and was co-chair of their 2005 quilt show. Aside from quilting for family and friends, Sue has designed and sewn several banners and quilts for her church. She is currently leading a ladies group in creating a quilt celebrating the church's 150th anniversary. She even gave the young people of the church community a chance to create blocks for their own quilt.

Patti Welch

Pieced the Everyday Bed Quilt and the Everyday Table Topper

Another prolific quilter, Patti is the former co-owner of a quilt shop in Sussex County, N.J. Recently Patti, her husband, Don and children relocated from Ogdensburg, N.J. to Crossville, Tenn. Patti offers suggestions for simplifying instructions that are much appreciated. Her speed and accuracy in piecing is astounding. Patti was also a member of the Garden State Quilt Guild. More information about The Garden State Quilt Guild can be found at www.gardenstatequilters.com.

Jennifer Roth

Pieced the Holiday Tree Skirt, sewed the Holiday and Everyday Window Shades and Valances, sewed the Holiday and Everyday Tablecloths and the Reversible Holiday Napkins

A young mother and new quilter, Jennifer has lots of experience sewing clothing and home décor items. She lives in Mt. Tabor with her husband, Edel, and adorable 2-year old, Sofia. How she found time to help us with so many projects while caring for a toddler is truly amazing.

Carol Singer

Quilted the Holiday Bed Quilt

Carol lives in Perkasie, Pa. with her husband Dave. She has been machine quilting for others on her long arm for the last ten years. In addition, Carol is a quilt designer in her own right, developing a line of patterns for sale and working on a series of quilts for a book proposal at the moment. Recently she has begun hand dyeing fabrics and her gradated collections are beautiful. Barbara met Carol at The Fiber Alliance, an art quilt group they belong to, which meets monthly in southeastern Pennsylvania.